PSALM 139

A devotional & expository study

EDWARD J. YOUNG

PSALM 139

A devotional & expository study

EDWARD J. YOUNG
Professor of Old Testament
Westminster Theological Seminary
Philadelphia, Pennsylvania

THE BANNER OF TRUTH TRUST
78b Chiltern Street, London W1

First published 1965

© The Banner of Truth Trust 1965

Set in 11 on 13 point Garamond
and printed and bound in Great Britain by
Billing & Sons Limited, Guildford and London

To the Reader

*P*SALM 139 is a prayer of David in which he exalts the majesty of God. God is all-knowing and God is everywhere present. God knows David, and David cannot flee from His presence. To such a God David would submit himself entirely. Our age needs just the emphasis that this Psalm gives, for we have lost the sense of God's majesty. Hence, there is no fear of God before our eyes, and irreverence and even superstition occupy our thoughts. A careful study of this Psalm should convince us of our wickedness and cause us once again to bow in adoration before the one eternal God.

This little book is written for those who wish to study this matchless Psalm. Its one purpose is to get at the meaning of the Psalm and to allow the Psalm to speak for itself. Only then, when we have actually heard what the Psalm has to say, can we pray with the Psalmist: 'Search me, O God, and know my heart: try me, and know my thoughts: and see if there be any wicked way in me, and lead me in the way everlasting.'

Preliminary Note

THIS Psalm bears the heading 'To the chief musician, a Psalm of David'. The headings of the Psalms are very old and there is not sufficient reason for refusing to accept their trustworthiness. At the same time, the meanings of the headings are often obscure, and this in itself argues for their antiquity.

The word translated 'chief musician' may refer to the conductor (cf. 2 Chronicles 2:2, 18), and the word rendered 'Psalm' possibly signifies a hymn sung to the accompaniment of a musical instrument.

There are many problems encountered in the study of this Psalm which are not immediately germane to the purpose of this study. One problem, namely the formal relationship between this Psalm and the Atharvaveda, passages in Xenophon, Plutarch, and the Koran, does not enter into the purpose of this study and so is not discussed.

1. O Lord, thou hast searched me, and known me.

IF WE ask wherein the greatness of this Psalm lies, we find an answer in the first word, LORD. The Psalmist immediately directs our attention not to himself or to the situation in which he is, but to God. It is of God that he intends to speak and not of himself. Thus, the Psalm is a prayer, addressed to God, and the word LORD introduces the theme.

Throughout the Psalm David speaks of God. Three times he mentions God as the LORD (cf. verses 1, 4 and 21); twice as GOD (vs. 17); once as Oh! God (vs. 19). Two different words for God are used, and these have particular significance. What is of interest is the fact that in the entire Psalm the common word for God (elohim) is not found. There is a reason why David employs different divine designations, and we shall consider these at the proper place.

David addresses God directly, plunging us right away into the subject of his thoughts. The word LORD sets the key, as it were, for all that follows. It remains and overshadows all that David has to say later. Throughout the Psalm we cannot forget the LORD, for He is the great central subject of which the Psalm is to speak. All else is secondary; here it is God and God alone who stands out supreme, and who is also to fill all our thoughts.

The expression LORD is of particular interest, and when David uttered it he spoke as one conscious of the sacredness and preciousness of the word. Much has been written about the meaning of this name, and there is much about it that is mysterious. If we try to discover the word's etymology, we plunge ourselves into great difficulty. There are, however, certain things that can be said. This is the name which God revealed to Moses at the burning bush, and that revelation was made in answer to a question which Moses had asked. When God appeared in the burning bush, He declared to Moses that He was the God of Moses' father, and that He had heard the cry of His people who then were in Egyptian bondage. Moses, however, had hesitated, and had told God that the people would want to have some mark or sign of identification. They would ask, 'What is his name?' (Exodus 3: 13), and Moses was at a loss as to what he should reply.

In answer to this question God then revealed His Name, and this He did in wondrous fashion. Speaking from the midst of the burning bush, He declared, 'I am that I am', thus asserting His eternity. Although times might change, and the purposes of God might seem to be forgotten, yet God abides the same. What He has promised will in His own time most certainly find fulfilment. He is the eternal God, and He can carry out and bring to fruition all His purposes and plans. He who spake to Moses was 'I AM', infinitely exalted above the gods of Egypt and the purposes of man. Against this background he gave to man His Name, the LORD, a word which in the Hebrew reflects upon the statement, 'I am that I am'.

The actual word itself, however, had already been known; what was not known was its significance. In the sixth chapter of Exodus (verse 3) God says to Moses, 'And I appeared to Abraham, to Isaac and to Jacob, as EL SHADDAI, but by my name the LORD was I not known to them'. What is meant is that the patriarchs, Abraham, Isaac and Jacob, had known God in the character of EL SHADDAI but not in the character of the LORD. As EL SHADDAI they had known him as the all-powerful God. It was as God Almighty that He had revealed Himself to them. When it had seemed to the patriarchs that the promises could not be fulfilled, then God displayed His power, and what was impossible with man was shown to be possible with God. The entire period of the patriarchs was one characterized by the power of God. All had seemed to conspire against the accomplishment of the promises; the patriarchs were impotent; they could do nothing. The feeble attempts of Abraham and Jacob, for example, to accomplish what God had promised, made clear that man could not perform the work of salvation. For that work almighty power was needed, and that power was provided by God at the appropriate time. God showed Himself to be almighty, a true EL SHADDAI. Thus the patriarchs had known him. They had not known Him, however, as the LORD.

Although this word which we have rendered LORD does reflect upon the name I AM, nevertheless, it also points to God as one who is a covenant God and who manifests that fact by acts of redemption and deliverance. At the time Israel had been in Egyptian bondage and servitude, and yet God chose her to be His people. Passing by other nations, more great and worthy, He nevertheless set His affection upon this weak slave people and chose it to be His own in order that, through this nation, His purposes of salvation and blessing might be made known to the entire world. 'The Lord did not set his love upon you, nor choose you, because ye were more in number than any people; for ye were the fewest of all people; But because the Lord loved you, and because he would keep the oath which he had sworn unto your fathers, hath the Lord brought you out with a mighty hand, and redeemed you out of the house of bondmen, from the hand of Pharaoh king of Egypt. Know therefore that the Lord thy God, he is God, the faithful God, which keepeth covenant and mercy with them that love him and keep his commandments to a thousand generations' (Deuteronomy 7: 7–9).

In these words the essence of the matter is clearly set forth. A covenant is simply a dispensation of sovereign grace imposed upon a people by God Himself. The Name which reminds that God is a covenant God is this word which we have translated the LORD. Although the patriarchs knew God as powerful and almighty they did not know Him as a covenant nor as a redeemer God. The Israelites were but bondslaves. Yet God chose them to be His people, and the essence of the covenant which He made with them was that they were to be God's people and in turn He would be their God. This relationship He showed in that He immediately did something for His people, delivering them from the bondage in which they found themselves. To Moses and the Israelites there was granted a revelation which the patriarchs had not been permitted to receive. No longer is God dealing with His people as with individuals; now He is ready to form them into a nation, the people of God, and hence, the covenant name, LORD, is revealed to them. To speak of God as the LORD is to speak of Him as Israel's God. This is the Name through which there is access to God; this is the Name which blazons abroad the fact that God has chosen Israel. Israel is His people in a sense which is true of no other nation.

David can thus begin the Psalm with an appeal to the One who is his own God. He can address God as the LORD. In this address there is tenderness and intimacy, but there is no irreverence. The privilege of addressing God as LORD is one which no man of himself can rightly take upon his lips. No one is entitled so to speak to the holy God but those to whom God has granted this privilege. And to David He had granted it; to David and to all those with whom He has entered into covenant. Only those, however, who are members of the covenant may so address God and be assured that He will hear them. This Psalm therefore is spoken by one with whom God had entered into covenant; one whom God had sovereignly chosen to be His own; one with whom He had been pleased to establish close relationship. And only those can follow David in thus addressing God, who like David are the objects of God's choice. None but God's people can call Him Lord, and no man calleth Him LORD save through Jesus Christ His Son.

David has placed the word LORD first in the Psalm and thus has emphasized it. He now proceeds to make a statement about the Lord. His great theme is LORD, but having stated the theme, he goes on to say, still addressing the Lord, 'Thou hast searched me and thou hast known'. It is possible to render the language 'thou dost search me and thou knowest', but probably, when we consider the whole context of the Psalm, it is better to translate by the past. David is referring to something that has already occurred. God knows David at the time when the Psalmist speaks to Him.

The first verb implies that God has engaged in an exhaustive search in order to learn all that there is to know about David. Basically the word means 'to dig'. Thus, Job says of God, 'He setteth an end to darkness, and searcheth out all perfection: the stones of darkness, and the shadow of death' (Job 28: 3). Here, however, the original sense of dig is not apparent, and all the word means is that there has been a minute and thorough examination and investigation on God's part. 'Then did he see it,' we read again in the same chapter of Job, 'and declare it; he prepared it, yea, and searched it out' (Job 28: 27). Again Job asks, 'Is it good that he should search you out?' (Job 13: 9).

David himself has been the object of this exhaustive examination. 'Thou hast searched ME', he says, and then, as a result of this searching, 'Thou knowest'. The Psalmist makes a general statement; He does not declare, 'Thou knowest me', but merely 'Thou knowest', and this is stronger and more forceful than if he had included the personal pronoun as an object, 'Thou knowest me'.

Whatever there is to know, God knows. This is the truth which he will enunciate concerning God, for it is not his purpose to speak to God as some abstract being who has no relationship with man, but rather to show that God knows him as an individual.

The two simple utterances sum up or present as a heading the thought which the Psalmist wishes to enlarge. It is his purpose to proceed with a discussion of the particulars, to show that God knows every detail of his life. Before he can turn to these details, however, he must state the theme with which he wishes to deal. He wishes to show that God is omniscient, and this with respect to himself.

What is meant, however, by the declaration, 'Thou hast searched me and thou knowest'? Does the Psalmist mean to assert that God was ignorant of David and could only come to know David after a long and exhausting examination? That would be true of us. We do not know a person upon first meeting; indeed, it is only after long contact with someone that we come to know him, if at all. What little we may learn of a person comes to us not right away but only after a long period of experience. Is this the case with God? Must God also engage in a particular study of someone so that He may know that person?

Fortunately for us that is not the case. If it were God could not truly be omniscient. If God were ignorant, He would not be the God of the Bible. We could not then speak of Him as the all-knowing God nor could we really have confidence in Him. It is not this, however, which David means. The language of the Psalm does not mean that God, being ignorant, must remove His ignorance by investigation. It means, rather, that God possesses full knowledge of David. Indeed, what the Psalm presents is only a vivid way of saying that God knows all that can be known of David. Had the Psalmist been writing a theological treatise he would have said that God was omniscient with respect even to Himself. He is not doing that, however; he is writing beautiful poetry, and hence expresses himself in a language that all can understand. He who reads the Psalm sympathetically will not miss its meaning. He will not entertain any low view of God but will rejoice in such a strong declaration of God's great and mighty knowledge.

Yet when one speaks of God he must utter the truth. If ever one must be careful in speaking, it is when he talks of God. To misrepresent God by saying what is not true about Him is to do a sinful thing. What warrant then did the Psalmist possess for thus speaking of the omniscient God?

Various answers have been given to this question, but there is one which we may briefly consider, for at the present time it is rather widespread. The Bible, we are told, is God's Word to man. In the Bible we hear the voice of the living God. Throughout we listen to what God has to say to us. In the Psalms, however, the case is different. Here in the Psalms we have the response of the devout heart to God. Hence, what the Psalmist is here declaring reflects the devotion and consecration of his own heart.

At first sight this statement seems to be quite helpful, but upon a little reflection, we believe, it must be abandoned. What warrant do we have for singling out the book of Psalms as the response of man to God, whereas we continue to assert that in the remainder of the Bible God speaks to man? And is not such a position in flat contradiction with what the Holy Spirit says through the apostle Paul when He declares that 'All Scripture is God-breathed' (2 Timothy 3: 16a)? Inasmuch as the Psalms are a part of Scripture they too must be regarded as God-breathed. Hence, the utterances of the Psalms and so of this particular Psalm must be understood as God-breathed Scripture and not merely the utterances of some devout and pious soul of the Old Testament age. And it is well that this is so! For, if these profound statements were merely the best that men could produce, then we could never be sure whether they were really trustworthy. If the 'Thou hast searched me and thou hast known' is nothing more than the sincere conviction of David, then, much as we admire David, we could never be sure that what was said here was the absolute truth. We could never have a certainty that God had also searched us and known us. We might indeed admire the profundity of the great thought pronounced, but we could never possess an absolute assurance that it actually was the truth. And, great as David was, we might very well wonder and question how he could have attained to such knowledge of God unless God Himself had revealed that knowledge to him. It is well then that the Scripture itself speaks out against such an unbiblical view of the Psalms. Much more comforting is the teaching which the Bible gives. The one hundred and thirty-ninth Psalm is Scripture, and hence is God-breathed. What we are considering in this remarkable 'Thou hast searched me and thou hast known' is not an utterance which found its origin in the heart of man, not even a devout man like David, but rather a blessed truth which God the Holy Spirit made known to His servant David. We therefore may read, and we may believe and be comforted. What David has here stated concerning himself is true also of us. God is our God and He knows us.

2. *Thou knowest my downsitting and mine uprising, thou understandest my thought afar off.*

H AVING stated that the LORD is omniscient, and that this omniscience has respect to himself, the Psalmist proceeds to indicate in what respect God knows him. First, however, he reverts to his principal subject, namely, the LORD, and again begins with an emphatic word, THOU. Before proceeding to point out in what respect God's omniscience may be seen he would once more have his readers contemplate the ONE to whom he is speaking. His is a God-centred prayer. Rather than attract attention to himself, he prefers that attention to rest upon God. It is enough that he can say THOU, for in this one word there is concentrated the essence of true prayer.

Not everyone can say THOU to God, for not everyone knows God. Only those who know God can thus address Him, for the word indicates the fact that the one who prays stands in intimate relationship with the One to whom he prays. To utter the word THOU is to acknowledge that God is a Person to whom one may speak and who will hear one's words. It is to say in effect that there is but one God, and that this God is capable of

hearing prayer and of fulfilling the desires of the suppli-
ant. The word sums up within itself the entirety of
theology, for the one who utters it must pray as a suppli-
ant, and in its very utterance give expression to the truth
that the God addressed is almighty whereas the one who
prays is but a weak creature. If we can say THOU to
God, we have rejected any belief in idols and we know
that the One to whom we speak is God and God alone.

Is there need to say more than THOU? If we can thus
address God, need we add thereto? Can we not rest in
this one truth alone? Of course we can so rest, but the
Psalmist is desirous of magnifying the greatness of the
God whom he thus reverently addresses. Hence, he
reverts to the thought with which he had concluded the
preceding verse. 'Thou knowest', he had declared, and
this thought calls to mind the similar expression which
Hannah had included in her prayer, 'For the LORD is a
God of knowledge, and by him actions are weighed'
(1 Samuel 2 : 3). The one whom the Psalmist so confidently addresses as LORD and THOU is not some being
far removed from the affairs of man's earthly life, but one
who possesses knowledge of man.

It is a comforting thought, for man in himself does not
possess knowledge. Man gropes about as though walking
in darkness. His way is beset on all sides with problems
that press in upon him and clamour for a solution. To
these problems man can often turn but an uncomprehend-
ing glance, for he has no knowledge to apply to their
solution. Professing to know and also to be wise,
nevertheless he does not know, and hence his decisions
and judgments are not those of wisdom and knowledge.

With God, however, knowledge is to be found, as well as the ability to apply this knowledge. God is all-knowing and God is all-wise. To be able to address such a God is a blessing indeed. Happy are those who can say THOU to a God of knowledge. They possess a treasure that cannot be matched upon this earth where darkness and ignorance reign.

What however is it that God knows? He knows the Psalmist's sitting down and rising up. Sitting down may refer either to the act of sitting or to the posture of the Psalmist in reclining or resting, and rising up may designate either the act of standing, arising from a sitting position, or the condition of standing. It is difficult to tell precisely what is intended. What is clear is that this sharp contrast refers to the entirety of David's life. The contrast seems to be made for the purpose of setting rest and motion over against one another. In other words, the reference is to all the postures and attitudes of man when he is awake.

During the course of our daily life we may easily forget God. Our lives are varied. At times we are active, standing up, walking, even running. At other times we are quiet, sitting down or relaxing. We engage in thought and meditation. Different activities give variety to life. One thing after another occupies the thoughts and attention, and we may live engrossed in the things of the moment, forgetting that God is with us. Yet He knows all of our life, every moment, every posture, every activity. At no time are our ways hidden from Him. When we relax and our minds engage in quiet thought, God knows. When we are busy with the cares of this life and our minds may forget Him, He knows. It is not possible to escape from Him. God knows all our lives.

Not only is the outward course of life known to Him, but also the thoughts of our hearts. The word which is translated 'thought' probably refers to the purpose or aim of a man's heart. Perhaps we may best express the original if we translate by the English word 'intention'. The purposes and intentions which arise in our hearts are known to God. This is striking, for we ourselves often do not know, much less understand, the intentions which come from our hearts. God not merely knows of these intentions; He understands them. The word is strong, and suggests that God knows all about these intentions. What their origin is, why they have arisen in our hearts, how they affect us: all this is perfectly understood by God. God understands, so we may bring out the thought, and this understanding manifests itself with respect to our thoughts.

Perhaps, although one cannot be sure, there is a certain gradation in the usage of the verbs. Not only does God know, but He also understands. At least, whether there is gradation of thought or not, the two verbs taken together suggest the most penetrating kind of knowledge. It is not a mere knowledge about David, but an intimate, thorough knowing and understanding all that there is to know about him. Such attributes can belong to God alone. No man can know as God knows; no man can possess the understanding of God. We know in part, and at best our knowledge is but a stammering of the truth. God's knowledge is perfect and all-embracing. Of Him alone may it be said that He knows and He understands.

All too often the intentions that arise in our hearts are not fully or even partially understood by ourselves. The advice of Socrates, 'know thyself', is well enough given, but how can we know ourselves? At best we have but a general idea of our purposes and intentions. Exhaustive knowledge belongs to God alone. There is One who does know and does understand us. Our ways may be hidden from ourselves, but they are not hidden from the knowledge of the One with whom we have to do.

What is meant, however, when the Psalmist declares that God knows or understands his intention from afar? Probably we may obtain a clue to the meaning by considering a verse in the previous Psalm, a Psalm which has many points of contact with this one. In verse 6, Psalm 138, we read, 'Though the LORD be high, yet hath he respect unto the lowly: but the proud he knoweth afar off'. Eliphaz the Temanite spoke in similar vein about God, 'Is not God in the height of heaven? and behold the height of the stars, how high they are! And thou sayest, How doth God know? can he judge through the dark cloud? Thick clouds are a covering to him, that he seeth not; and he walketh in the circuit of heaven' (Job 22: 12–14). Jeremiah brings out the same thought, 'Am I a God at hand, saith the LORD, and not a God afar off?' (Jeremiah 23: 23).

From these passages it would seem to be clear that by the term 'afar off' the Psalmist has in mind the thought that God is far removed from man in heaven. It is God's transcendence which is here in view. Although God is in heaven and not upon earth, nevertheless, from this far-off place, He has a perfect and complete knowledge and understanding of David's life, both external and internal. The phrase 'afar off', in other words, emphasizes the wonder and marvel of God's knowledge. A God who is at hand and who could therefore see with His own eyes, as it were, might be expected to know the Psalmist, but the knowledge of God is all the more wonderful when God is afar off. Man is upon earth; God is in heaven, and yet God has a fuller knowledge of man than man does of himself. 'The LORD is in his holy temple, the LORD's throne is in heaven: his eyes behold, his eyelids try, the children of men' (Psalm 11 : 4). The God of glory, the sovereign LORD, seated upon the heavenly throne, possesses perfect knowledge of man. How wondrous is such a God! Indeed, we must note that every word in the verse is designed to point to the majesty and greatness of the God of whom David speaks.

At the same time there is a danger that we may completely misunderstand the language of the Psalmist. The words 'afar off' are striking and they are true; God is indeed afar off. This is a truth which must never be minimized nor denied. In theological language we should speak of God's transcendence. God is in heaven: He is not to be brought down and identified with His creation, but reigns above His creation in supreme majesty.

This does not mean, however, that God has nothing to do with His creation. Although He has brought all things into existence by the Word of His power, and although He exists in absolute independence of all that He has created, nevertheless He governs and preserves all His creatures and all their actions. We cannot escape from His presence. At this particular point, however, the Psalmist desires to emphasize the transcendence of God. God, who is in heaven, knows me more intimately than I know myself. His knowledge is infinite, eternal and unchangeable. I am the object of that infinite divine knowledge. This is the matchless truth that David desires to express.

3. *Thou compassest my path and my lying down, and art acquainted with all my ways.*

ONE OF the incomparable excellencies of the Bible is to be found in its superb literary quality, and one of the factors which contributes to this literary quality is variety. Like the revelation of God in the world about us, so His revelation in the Bible is varied. Just as we do not meet a monotonous sameness in the world in which we live, but rejoice in its wondrous change, so also in the Bible we meet with a variety of expression that ever calls forth wonder and ever enchants. Of course the most important characteristic of the Bible is not its literary quality, superb as that is. The most important characteristic is the fact that the Bible is the Word of God. God, however, did not give to man an uninteresting revelation, but one rich in variety and which confronts man with the truth in diverse ways.

The Psalmist, therefore, in this present verse, does not merely repeat the form which he had previously used. He has already focused our attention upon God and deflected attention from himself. For this reason he may now vary his manner of statement, without in the least turning our thoughts away from God. Hence, in place of beginning this verse with a repeated THOU, he varies his method and simply states, 'My path and my lying down thou hast sifted'. It is an interesting variation; in the preceding verse the Psalmist had put his stress upon THOU, and almost casually added the references to himself; here, he simply continues with those references, and leads us naturally to a consideration of 'my path and my lying down'. The path is the way in which one must travel during his active life, since life in the Bible is often conceived as a journey. For all practical purposes the word is an equivalent of the expression 'my rising up' which David had just employed in the preceding verse.

To indicate the passive life the Psalmist speaks of 'my lair' or 'my place of lying down'. The two expressions, however, are not mere synonyms of the phrases in the second verse. In that verse David had mentioned his lying down and his rising up. Now, to designate the entirety of his life, he speaks of his path and the place of his repose. Different figures thus serve to express the fullness of life, as though to stress the fact that God knows wholly and completely the life of David, no matter from what aspect it be considered.

A certain beauty and strength of expression may also be seen in that David uses his language in a chiastic arrangement. What this means will be clear if we note that in verse two he considered first the passive life and then the active, whereas in verse three he first mentions the active and then the passive life. A diagram will bring out this point.

Verse 2.   My sitting down $\diagdown\diagup$ My rising up
Verse 3.   My path $\diagup\diagdown$ My lying down.

This arrangement, which we might designate as ab—ba, is very frequent in the Old Testament, and lends strength and dignity of expression. It is in the use of this simple device that so much of the power of expression of the Old Testament resides. In saying this, however, we must be cautious. Without a doubt the literary devices which find employment in the Hebrew of the Old Testament go a long way to giving a majesty and might to its expressions. The real majesty of the Old Testament, however, which gives it its grandeur, is found primarily not in its literary nature, wondrous and superb as that is, but in the message which the Old Testament presents. Great and mighty as is the literary aspect of the Word of God, it is the Word of God itself which is quick and powerful, and sharper than any two-edged sword. Yet we must ever be grateful to God that in revealing to us His matchless Word He gave a Word of such supreme literary beauty.

To state the truth that God has thoroughly searched out and examined his path and his lair David employs what may be called picture language. The verb which he uses means to winnow, and thus David takes from everyday life in Palestine a figure which would be rich in meaning for his hearers or readers. To the dwellers in Palestine winnowing would have been thoroughly familiar. The worker throws the grain high into the air, and the wind blows or carries away the chaff, leaving the true grain to fall to the ground. Thus, the wind separated between the chaff and the grain. It is this beautiful figure which David employs of God. God has winnowed his path and his lying down, so that that path and lying down have been thoroughly examined and searched out by God.

God has tested them. Thus, by means of another figure we are brought again face to face with the truth that God knows the life of David.

That there may be no misunderstanding of his thought, the Psalmist inserts the phrase, 'and all my ways'. The language is self-explanatory. All that David does, all that he suffers, all of his actions and all that affects him, is known to God. Again, he uses variety in his choice of expression. He employs a verb which implies use or habit. In Numbers 22: 30 we read, 'Have I ever shown the habit of doing thus to thee?' The word suggests an acquaintance which results from familiarity and habit. It would not be incorrect to translate 'to know intimately'. God intimately knows all the ways of David. This is more than the Psalmist can say of himself; it is more than can be said of any mere man. Man at best seems to be a bundle of contradictions; he does not know himself as he should; he is not always sure of himself; he cannot in every instance tell why he acts as he does. He is unaware of the thousands of influences that for good or evil affect his actions. God, on the other hand, possesses an intimate knowledge and understanding of man which extends to every detail of his life.

4. For there is not a word in my tongue, but, lo, O LORD, thou knowest it altogether.

DAVID now proceeds to give an illustration of the truth which he has been declaring. This is done by means of the introductory 'for'. We might paraphrase the thought: 'God possesses an intimate knowledge of all my ways, as may be seen in the fact that He knows the word upon my tongue.' Or, 'God knows me intimately, for, to take an example, He knows the word upon my tongue'. To declare that the word is in the tongue is to say that it is in the power of the tongue. The word is now ready to be spoken. The tongue has taken hold of that word, and is about to declare it.

Men do not always know what they are going to say. Indeed, thoughtful utterance is extremely difficult, and often, when a man begins to speak, he himself is ignorant of the words that will flow from his mouth. It is not so with God, however. The speech of man is not unknown to Him. Even before man utters his words, while they are yet upon the tongue, unspoken, the Lord knows them. This is not to say that God has merely a general idea of what a man will speak, but rather that God actually knows the individual words which the speaker is to use before he speaks them forth.

The relation between the two halves of the sentence is quite interesting. We might translate, 'For there is not a word upon my tongue, which thou dost not know', or 'For there is not a word upon my tongue, (but) thou knowest it utterly'. Probably the latter relationship is to be preferred. Actually there are two independent statements in the verse, and the second is equal in importance to the first.

David begins the second statement with the interjection, 'Behold!' and it is an interjection designed to call the Lord's attention to what he is about to utter. Conceivably there is somewhat of dismay in the Psalmist's tone as he speaks, for there is no escape from the omniscience of God. Indeed, there is not even a word upon my tongue, he says, behold! thou knowest it. It is as though he is confessing to God that there is nothing that he can hide from God. This God is unlike the gods of the nations which cannot hear nor speak. He possesses a knowledge of man from which man cannot hide. 'Thou knowest it altogether,' David says to the Lord. Why should I even try to speak a word without Thee? Whatever word comes upon my tongue, see, I cannot hide it from Thee.

Hence, the Psalmist speaks to God, addressing Him as LORD, and declares plainly and frankly that God knows his words altogether. The last word of the verse may be rendered 'all of it', and it either means that God knows the words altogether or else He knows every bit of the words that appear upon David's tongue. Whichever of these two renderings we adopt we may see that the language does teach that God knows in their fullness and entirety the words which are upon David's tongue.

Certainly God knows every word, but more than that He knows the words in their entirety.

The words which come upon our tongues are the expression of the thoughts that have been formed in our hearts. Both the thoughts and words are known to God. How practical is this truth of God's omniscience! From men we may be able to conceal the thoughts which we have. And it is well that this is so. Thoughts of anger, jealousy, hatred; how good it is that other men need not know them. The wicked thoughts that from time to time find lodgment in our hearts we may hide from men. From God, however, we cannot conceal them. For this reason we must guard the heart, for out of it are the issues of life. Should thoughts of evil reign in our hearts, they may break forth into expression in words of evil. None of this can be kept hidden from God, who knows us for what we are. The deep contemplation of this truth will strengthen us that we keep our hearts pure from evil and our lips from speaking guile.

5. Thou hast beset me behind and before, and laid thine hand upon me.

*T*HE Hebrew word order differs from the English: 'Behind and before thou hast beset me'. The language contains an almost imperceptible transition from the consideration of God's omniscience to that of His omnipresence. Indeed, it would seem that the former arises from the latter. If David would go forward God is present; should he step backward as though to flee, yet God is there. In whatever direction he turns he cannot escape from the all-knowing God.

The development of thought is natural and brings to the fore the question, 'Why should one desire to escape from the presence of God?' 'Why should reflection upon God's omniscience lead one to seek escape from Him?' These questions are legitimate. When we think of God as He has revealed Himself to us in His Word, we are at once reminded of the great gulf which separates the Creator from the creature. In our daily lives we do not meditate upon God as we ought. Our lives are so filled with activity that in this modern day we have all but abandoned the practice of meditation. We are activists, and have allowed that fact to crowd God out from our thoughts. We do not take the time to meditate upon Him as we should.

When, however, we turn aside from the cares and demands of daily activity and enter into the quiet of meditation we are brought face to face with the greatness of our God. He is not a man like ourselves, whom we can measure and circumscribe with the measures and limits which we apply to ourselves. Instead, He is so great that we cannot comprehend Him. We cannot bring Him down and place Him under the microscope of the human mind. Whereas we are limited and circumscribed, we learn from Scripture that God is not limited. He is the infinite One. Hence, we are not able to think of Him as He is in Himself. There is nothing in this earth with which we can compare Him, for this earth and its fullness belong to Him as His creation. God, however, in all of His perfections and attributes is infinite, eternal and unchangeable. Hence, when we think of His omniscience, we tremble. Before such a God who can stand? From this God there is no escape. Before Him we can only bow in adoration and in genuine reverence.

David does not contradict what he had stated before, that God understands his thought from afar. God in heaven is truly afar, yet God is also omnipresent. Theologians are on good Biblical ground when they speak both of the transcendence and immanence of God. God is everywhere, and yet God is the mighty Creator, whose dwelling is in the heaven. These are truths which our finite minds cannot comprehend nor reconcile, but we must note that the Bible teaches both God's omnipresence and also His transcendence. There is, however, an error which we must avoid. God is truly everywhere, as this Psalm makes clear. At the same time we must not fall into the error of thinking that He is to be identified with His creation. This is the error of pantheism, and we must be on our guard against it. God and His creation are not one; they are not to be identified. The summer day, the glorious sunset, the flower of the field, the love of a mother for her child: these are not God. In them God's working is seen, for He upholds the world by the word of His power, but He is not Himself the same as His creation. God's providence is one thing, but that God and His creation are one is something quite different. The Bible teaches divine providence. God does indeed uphold and govern all His creatures and all their actions. But the Bible does not teach pantheism. God and His creatures are not one. That God is to be identified with creation is an error which can lead only to eternal death; that God is omnipresent is a blessed truth of the Bible which will lead one to a deeper love for, and a greater devotion to, the mighty God of the Scriptures.

To express the thought of inescapability from God David uses a word that actually means 'to shut up' or 'to enclose'. God has confined man by shutting him up so that whether man go forward or backward he is hemmed in and unable to flee from God. All about him is the LORD, from whose presence he can find no escape.

Possibly, however, if one soared upward and looked above, he might find a way to flee from the omnipresent God. Such a thought might occur to a person, but God has placed His hand upon David, in order that there be no flight upward. The language is graphic, and speaks of the palm of the hand. Thus we have the picture of the outstretched palm of God placed over David, so that David is held down and cannot escape. Actually, the figure of the hand suggests being in someone's power. Job, for example, has used the figure in the words, 'Neither is there any daysman betwixt us, that might lay his hand upon us both' (Job 9: 33), and also 'Withdraw thine hand far from me: and let not thy dread make me afraid' (Job 13: 21). 'Behold, my terror shall not make thee afraid, neither shall my hand be heavy upon thee' (Job 33: 7).

When God places His almighty hand upon a person, that person is completely in His power, and it is this truth which David is compelled to recognize. What the Psalmist here says, however, applies to all men without exception. There are none that can escape from God's presence, for He is everywhere.

6. Such knowledge is too wonderful for me; it is high, I cannot attain unto it.

THE THOUGHTS which the Psalmist has just expressed lead him to utter an exclamation of wonder at the greatness and incomprehensibility of God's knowledge. Hence he breaks out with the word 'Wonderful', uttering this word before anything else in the sentence. Indeed, it is this remarkable word which colours all that follows. There is a similar sentence in Isaiah 9: 6, where the prophet mentions the Name of the Messiah. The first element in the Name is the word WONDER, and that word overshadows all to follow, raising it to the sphere of the incomprehensible and the divine. Indeed, the word which Isaiah uses is very closely related to this word of David's. It is spelled almost identically, and is based upon the three root letters of the present word.

The underlying idea of the word is that of separateness or distinctness. The root is used of the miracles which God performed when He brought the Israelites out of Egyptian bondage. These great miracles were acts of God, performed by His supernatural power in the external world, and as they appeared to man were distinct from the ordinary providential working of the Lord. The knowledge which David now wishes to praise is distinct and separate from human knowledge; it is divine. We perhaps may best understand the force of the word by comparing a somewhat similar usage in Judges 13: 18. In this remarkable passage the Angel of the Lord had appeared to Manoah and his wife, and Manoah asks after the Name of the Angel. The reply is not a rebuke, but a design to show Manoah that the name of the Angel is an incomprehensible Name. In this sense it is wonderful or Divine. Whereas Manoah might know the mere vocable by which to address God, yet the reply of the Angel was intended to show that the actual Name itself was Divine. It was hidden from man in the sense that it was incomprehensible to him. So it is with the knowledge of which David now speaks. Such knowledge is incomprehensible; it is something that man cannot possess, for man is but a creature and hence finite; the knowledge of which David here speaks belongs to an infinite being. Hence, man cannot possess it.

The Hebrew text may be translated, 'Wonderful is knowledge from me', and this short sentence means, 'Such knowledge is too wonderful for me to possess'. Of what knowledge, however, is David speaking? Does David have in mind man's knowledge of God? It would not seem so, for this man already possesses. Rather, the knowledge of which the Psalmist here speaks is one which the Psalmist himself cannot have. It is the knowledge possessed by God, the knowledge of an infinite being. It is an incomprehensible knowledge not for God but for man. Hence David cannot attain to it; it is 'from him', i.e. it is that which he cannot attain unto. Were we to employ theological terms, we should say that the knowledge is transcendent.

And yet the Psalmist does not actually say 'thy knowledge'. He contents himself with the simple term 'knowledge', for it is this which fills his thought with awe. Perhaps the mere term is more forceful than the phrase 'God's knowledge'. 'Wonderful!' he breathes out, giving to that first word all the tremendous emphasis and stress that is its due, 'wonderful is knowledge!' Yet these words are spoken after the repeated statements concerning God's omniscience. Can there be any serious doubt that David is speaking of God's knowledge?

Man's knowledge of an object must always be the knowledge of a creature. What man possesses is simply a finite understanding. He cannot have an exhaustive knowledge nor an absolute penetration or understanding of any given object, for his own mind is finite and hence limited in capacity to know and to understand. God's knowledge is that of the infinite One; man's that of a finite being. The two are distinct and cannot be identified any more than the creature and Creator can be identified.

When David thus exalts the knowledge of God, he does not mean to assert that he himself can have no knowledge. He does have knowledge, in so far as he thinks the revealed thoughts of God after Him. But David's knowledge is only a reflection, as it were, of God's knowledge. David knows in part, but he does know; his knowledge and ours also are simply that which the creature possesses. The knowledge of God, he continues, is high, and this term signifies that man cannot attain unto it, for it is beyond man's reach. This word of course is not to be taken in a mere physical sense, as though the knowledge of God could be attainable to David if it were merely on the earth with him. What the language means is that the knowledge of God is such that only God can possess it; hence, it cannot be reached by man. Man can no more attain unto the knowledge which God possesses than he can become God Himself.

Lastly, David makes the confession, 'I cannot attain unto it'. If we examine his language carefully we note that he omits the word 'attain' and actually says only, 'I cannot unto it'. God's knowledge is incomprehensible. It is knowledge such as no mere man can possibly possess, for it belongs to God alone. Indeed, the purpose of the language is to show that man and God are distinct. David wishes to make it clear not merely that God is above man, but that He is infinitely above man.

Such an emphasis is eminently needed in our day, for men tend to bring God down to the human level. They speak of God with familiarity, as though He were simply one of themselves. The sense of awe and wonder in the presence of God has all but disappeared. Men speak of God with flippancy; His Name no longer brings fear to the heart. It is well then that we pause to remember that God is our Creator. We need Him; He does not need us. He made us and He exists independent of us. We are dependent upon Him, and without Him we can do nothing. The very breath of our lives belongs to Him and He can take it from us when He will.

There is no third party to whom we may go, no intermediary who will judge between God and ourselves.

It is to Him alone that we belong, and we are subject to Him in all our ways. David's language stresses these important and much-needed truths. In discussing God's omniscience David is showing that God and man are utterly distinct. The line between God the Creator and man the creature must never be broken down; indeed, it cannot be broken down, although man constantly tries to break it and to obliterate it. God, however, is not subject to man's desires; man is subject to God.

Does David fall into despair when he realizes that God's knowledge is impossible for him to possess? Such might seem to be the case, but it is not so, for David proceeds to the contemplation of what he has just introduced, God's omnipresence. Far from falling into despair, David rejoices in the truth concerning God, and this rejoicing of heart manifests itself in the thoughts which he proceeds to utter.

Throughout our discussion we have been speaking of David the Psalmist, and we have regarded the thoughts expressed in this Psalm as the thoughts which the Spirit of God has spoken through the mouth of his servant David. This is in accordance with what the heading of the Psalm itself has to say. In the heading we read that this is a Psalm by David. It is true that some students of the Bible believe that this statement in the heading does not actually intend to attribute the authorship of the Psalm to David, but that it merely wishes to assert that the Psalm is composed after the model of David's Psalms. There is a reason why some Bible students and scholars have hesitated to acknowledge that the Psalm was composed by David. That is because of the presence of what are called

Aramaisms in the Psalm. What, however, is an Aramaism?
The Aramaic language is closely related to the Hebrew in
which the Old Testament is written. It used to be held
that only late in their history did the Hebrews have any
real contact with those who spoke Aramaic. For this
reason, it was claimed, whenever we find an Aramaic
word in the Old Testament or a Hebrew word that is
spelled in Aramaic fashion or in some ways betrays an
Aramaic influence we can be sure that the Hebrew
passage in which this Aramaism is found is very late.

Is this position, however, correct? For a time most
people said that it was, and hence, because there are
several of these Aramaisms in this hundred and thirty-
ninth Psalm, many have refused to attribute the Psalm to
David as its human author. It is acknowledged that both
in its contents and in its poetic character the Psalm is in
every way worthy of David. Nevertheless, due to the
presence of these Aramaisms the Psalm is denied to
David.

Although the majority of Biblical scholars were thus
willing to deny the Psalm to David, nevertheless God
raised up a hero of the Faith who challenged the validity
of the assertion that the presence of an Aramaism in a
document proves that that document was late. This was
the late Robert Dick Wilson, a man who was willing for
the sake of Christ and His truth to live a comparatively
obscure life in order that he might devote his time to the
study and teaching of the Bible. In the quiet of his study
Dr Wilson examined minutely this claim that was made
about Aramaisms, and found that it was without founda-
tion. What Dr Wilson wrote on the subject is not easy to

read but it is worth reading. By adducing many an example he showed that when an Aramaism is found in a passage of the Old Testament that Aramaism proves nothing at all with respect to the date of the passage in question. Hence, even though there may be in the Psalm words which legitimately can be called Aramaisms, this in itself is no argument against the Davidic authorship of the Psalm.

The old argument is losing its force, however, and men are no longer pressing it with the strength and conviction that was once the case. Instead, some modern scholars, impressed with the remarkable statements in the Psalm concerning the all-knowing and omnipresent God, are asking, what was the origin of these thoughts? In answering their own question they are pointing to what they regard as somewhat similar statements found in Egypt, addressed to the sun god Amon-Re. On a papyrus, known as Papyrus Leiden 350, there is a fragment of a hymn to the sun god, and in this hymn there is an exaltation of his omniscience and omnipresence. This hymn is to be dated at quite an early time, and now it is being asserted that there may be an Egyptian influence present in the Psalm, and therefore it would be possible to date the Psalm at a comparatively early time.

The similarities between this Psalm and the statements of the hymn to the sun god, however, are of a merely formal kind. They are vastly overshadowed by the differences. It is not to Egypt that we need look for the source of these remarkable utterances concerning God. David was the recipient of divine revelation, and it is to such revelation alone that we must look. The Bible itself teaches this. In the fourth chapter of the book of Acts we read of God, 'Who by the mouth of thy servant David hast said' (vs. 25). In this prayer of the apostles they declare that God has spoken through the mouth of David His servant. This is the Scriptural explanation of the matter. Of course, there may be similar sounding expressions found in the religions of antiquity, but we must note that the sun god to whom these praises are uttered is a being without reality; he does not exist. The mere words of praise spoken to him are nothing more than mere words. Their surface similarities disappear before the tremendous differences which separate them from the divinely revealed words of the Bible.

Even though we cannot look to Egypt for the source of the thoughts expressed in this Psalm, nevertheless, the comparison with Egypt is interesting; for it shows how scholars can be influenced. For a time, the presence of Aramaisms was the determining factor; because of these Aramaisms, the Psalm had to be late. Now, however, little attention is paid to Aramaisms, and the influence of Egyptian religion is paramount. There is no reason, men now say, why the Psalm cannot be early. Our guide, however, should not be scholarship as such but rather simple dependence upon the statements of Scripture. The headings of the Psalms should not be rejected as untrustworthy. These headings are old, and we have every reason for trusting them. It was David, therefore, as the heading states, who acknowledged that he could not attain unto the knowledge of God.

7. *Whither shall I go from thy spirit? or whither shall I flee from thy presence?*

*T*HE contemplation of God's omniscience leads to a consideration of the possibility of escaping from God's presence. Hemmed in as he is by God, is there no way of escape? Why, however, should the Psalmist wish to flee from God? It may be that he is simply seeking to show in the abstract that it is not possible for any man to flee God's presence. More likely, however, it is the consciousness of his own sin that leads the Psalmist to ask whether he can escape God's presence. This seems to be supported by what is later given in the Psalm itself, where the Psalmist appeals to God to search him and see if there be any wicked way in him. As a sinner David would flee from God's presence either in order to escape from the judging hand of God or from the punishment which God would inflict upon him. The desire to flee from God is due to a realization of our own unworthiness and sinfulness.

In the garden of Eden Adam and Eve did the foolish thing of seeking to hide from the presence of God in the midst of the trees of the garden, and when God spoke to them, the first word of fallen man was: 'Thy voice I heard in the garden.' 'Thy voice'—it is that from which man would escape, were it possible. Today there are men who wish to hide from 'thy voice'. When they hear the voice of God, they seek to stifle and suppress every thought of Him. It is sin which leads us to do the foolish thing of trying to escape from God. From Him, however, there is no escape. Indeed, the only way to escape from Him is to flee to Him, for it is in Him alone that we find refuge from the punishment which our sins deserve.

The Psalmist does not expect an answer to his question. He knows that there is no place to which he can go where the Spirit of God will not also be present. God maintains the life of all things by His Spirit, who is active and vigorous, a power that works everywhere. Yet the Spirit is far more than a mere power. He is a Person. It is He who sustains life, and a mere impersonal power is not able to do this. Although David may not have understood the doctrine of the Holy Spirit in the fullness that was revealed in the New Testament, nevertheless, he did know that this Spirit of God was the One who kept alive all men and all that lives. Of this Spirit he might well have said that He was the Author and Giver of life. To speak of the Spirit of God, then, is to speak of One who is God. From the Spirit there is no escape.

To lend force to his question the Psalmist asks another, expressing essentially the same thought in parallel words. 'And whither from thy presence shall I flee?' The word which we have translated 'presence' actually refers to the face or countenance; it is as though David had said that he could not flee from before God's countenance. Wherever he goes God's countenance is before him. Perhaps there is somewhat of gradation in the verbs employed. First David speaks of going from God's Spirit and then of fleeing from His presence. Conceivably a person might seek to go away from God and be unable to do so. Could he not, however, flee from God? If he runs, travelling at a rapid pace, is there not more likelihood that he will escape from God? If mere going fails, will not fleeing succeed?

In using this parallel method of statement David is writing true Hebrew poetry. The poetry of the Old Testament is characterized by what we may call parallelism. To express his thoughts the Psalmist utters a statement once and then proceeds to repeat it in slightly different words. We may take almost any verse of the Psalms as an example. In the first verse of the twenty-fourth Psalm we read:

| The earth is the Lord's | and the fulness thereof, |
| The world | and they that dwell therein. |

In this verse the words 'the world' form a parallel to 'the earth', and 'they that dwell therein' a parallel to 'the fulness'. By means of this phenomenon of parallelism the Psalmist is able to impress his thoughts upon the mind of the hearer or reader. He also can lend vigour to his utterance. It is this which David does here. He utters this thought a second time, thus reinforcing it, but he also includes a certain gradation in his expression.

What answer do these questions of David demand? Clearly they require a negative answer. There is nowhere that a person can go where he can be free of God.

Wherever one is, there is God's Spirit also; wherever he flees, the Face of God beholds him. Who cannot but bow in praise and adoration before so great a God?

8. If I ascend up into heaven, thou art there: if I make my bed in hell, behold, thou art there.

*D*AVID considers some of the possibilities for escape from God's presence. Apparently when people spoke in Israel of escape they looked to the height and then to the depth. In Amos 9: 2 God considers Israel's sinners, and says, 'Though they dig into hell, thence shall mine hand take them; though they climb up to heaven, thence will I bring them down.' Neither hell nor heaven will provide an escape from God. David first mentions heaven, for it is the height which is supreme. If man should go to the highest height, can he not then find himself free of God? To ascend unto heaven or to scale heaven, is to go up to heaven. According to Genesis God created the heavens and the earth. Again, the firmament which God placed in the midst of the primaeval waters is called heaven. Heaven, therefore, is high above the earth, yet heaven will not provide an escape from God.

What happens should David succeed in ascending unto the heavens? The answer is abrupt: 'There art thou.' There, where David has ascended; there, that supposed place of escape; there, even there is God. Thou, O God art there. For David it had been a toilsome ascent. To scale heaven is no mean task; it would indeed surpass the powers of man; high as man could go, he could not reach the heaven. Should he, however, accomplish the impossible and reach that place, after so much toil and labour, there God is. How clearly this language stresses the omnipresence of God!

Can there not, however, be escape from God in the opposite direction? Cannot David descend even to the place where the departed spirits have gone, namely, Sheol, and so escape from God? Suppose he does that, suppose he makes even Sheol to be his couch, behold, there God is! This is the second time in the Psalm that in addressing God he has employed the word behold. It almost becomes a cry of despair.

How clearly this language brings out the infinite distinction between man the creature and God the Creator! God's omnipresence is shown by the simple statements, 'There art thou', and 'Behold thee!' God is in heaven and He is in Sheol. He is omnipresent. David, however, is not omnipresent. He is not in heaven; to be in heaven he must ascend there. David is not in Sheol; to be there he must descend and make his couch.

The contrast between God and David is striking. Also striking is the contrast between heaven and Sheol. In the Old Testament Sheol is regarded as the place of the dead, where the departed spirits have gone. As such it was conceived to be in the heart of the earth, far below earth's surface. In condemning the Babylonian king, Isaiah also has made a contrast between the height of heaven and the depth of Sheol. The king in his haughtiness had sought to be like the most High. He had boasted that he would ascend into the heights of heaven and exalt his throne above the stars of God. He would ascend above the heights of the clouds and be like the most High. Instead of this, however, he would be brought down to Sheol, to the very deepest places of the pit. Sheol, therefore, serves fittingly to indicate the opposite distance from heaven. As heaven is in the height, so Sheol is in the depth.

Perhaps there is also another contrast which should not be overlooked. Not only are heaven and Sheol separated by distance, but also in character. In heaven is the throne of God, and there are God's own with Him. Sheol, on the other hand, is the place where the wicked go and where they receive punishment. Yet, both, heaven and Sheol, are in God's control. He is present in both. In heaven He blesses His own; in Sheol He executes vengeance and punishment among those who are the children of wrath. Neither heaven nor Sheol can deliver from Him. He is omnipresent.

Yet there is something strange about David's language. Why should he speak of making Sheol his couch? Matthew Henry, that devout interpreter of the Bible, remarks that hell is a most uncomfortable place to make one's bed. David was doubtless well aware that Sheol was not the most comfortable place for a couch. Why, then does he speak in this manner? Possibly, the reason is that he simply desires to make a contrast. In mentioning heaven, he had spoken of action, namely, ascending to heaven. Ascending involved exertion. In Sheol, however, David would simply make his bed. This is not action, but repose. Whether David be active or whether he be in repose, wherever he is, there also is God. It is that which he is saying. In other words, wherever we are, be it in heaven or in hell, whether active or at repose, we cannot escape from God. His all-seeing eye is ever with us.

A very interesting parallel to this thought has come to light on some of the tablets discovered in Tell el-Amarna in Egypt. The story of the discovery is well known. In the year 1887 an Egyptian peasant working in a garden first came across these tablets. They have been studied and translated, and they contain correspondence between the kings of various Canaanitish cities and the great king of Egypt. On one of these tablets we read the following statements:

'Whether we ascend unto heaven,
Or we descend to the earth,
Our head is in thine hands.'

The language of this tablet is simply the exaggerated language of one who flatters the king, the reigning Pharaoh. Very different, however, is the language of the Psalm. David is not flattering God. He is speaking in profound reverence, deeply conscious of the fact that in reality and actually there is no escape from God's presence. The writer of the letter simply was praising the king, and asserting that he was in the king's power. Of course he did not take seriously the thought that if he ascended unto heaven, he would still be in the power of the Pharaoh, for what power did the Pharaoh have in heaven? We need not appeal to this tablet as the source of the thoughts which David utters in this verse. We can note, however, that the appearance of formally similar thoughts at such an early time shows that there can be no objection to considering this Psalm early and ascribing it to David.

9. If I take the wings of the morning, and dwell in the uttermost parts of the sea;

*A*SCENT to heaven and descent to Sheol provide no escape from God. What about travel in a horizontal direction? Should one go to the east or the west, can he not thus find an escape? We normally translate the Psalmist's language by a conditional sentence, but actually, the words are far stronger. It would be well to present a literal rendering of the Hebrew: 'I raise the wings of the morning, I would dwell in the uttermost part of the sea.' The abruptness of the clauses lends life and vigour to expression. Actually, the Psalmist is uttering a condition. What he means is that even if he should raise the wings of the morning, he could not flee from God's presence.

A minor question of interpretation arises. Some have said that one could not raise the wings of the morning, unless he first had wings to raise. Hence, they have preferred to translate the first verb: 'If I take the wings of the morning'. This translation is favoured because it is thought to be in accord with a later usage of the verb, and those who adopt it are largely influenced by the view that the Psalm is late. Such an argument is not valid. If one raise the wings of morning, it is to be assumed that he has the wings to raise. What is meant is that if the Psalmist should raise wings such as the morning possesses, even then he could not flee away from God's presence.

What are the wings of the morning? David employs an unusual word which refers to the dawn, and so it is actually the wings of the dawn that he has in mind. What, however, are these wings, and what is the purpose of his expression? One view is that the language simply designates the east as the place where the sun rises, and so stands in contrast with the west, the uttermost part of the sea. Another interpretation would see here a reference to speed. The wings of the morning spread out rapidly, and it is that thought of rapidity which the Psalmist is said to have in mind. The Psalmist, on this interpretation, is expressing the wish to fly with the speed of the early dawn as it covers the entire sky.

It is perhaps difficult to decide with any positiveness between these two positions, although in all probability the latter is to be preferred. Homer spoke of the rosy-fingered dawn, and it would seem that a similar thought is found here also. As one looks toward the east, there is first the appearance of faint light. Stronger and stronger it grows, and suddenly the rays of light, like long rosy fingers, stretch out to north and south. The sun then arises and light reigns upon the earth. Could David travel with the speed of the rosy fingers of dawn, even so he would not journey with sufficient speed to flee from God.

In the second member of the verse, however, he does turn his attention and thought to the west. The verb employed contains the thought of wishing to dwell, 'Oh!

that I could dwell!' or, 'I would dwell'. Again, there is the contrast between movement and repose. To travel with the wings of morning and to dwell stand in contrast the one to the other. David speaks of the farthermost part of the sea, by which he means as far as one can travel. It is the western extremity of the Mediterranean that is in mind. Journey as far west as one can, so the thought may be paraphrased, nevertheless, even here one does not go beyond the presence of God. God is found at the western extremity of the sea.

10. Even there shall thy hand lead me, and thy right hand shall hold me.

I N THE words of this verse the conclusion is given. Whether David raise the wings of the morning or whether he dwell in the farthermost part of the sea, even there, far as that place is from Jerusalem, God leads him with His hand. We note an almost imperceptible change of emphasis in the Psalm. The tone of fear before God seems to be dropped, and a note of comfort is introduced. True, there is no escape from God, but David in the farthermost part of the sea does not meet God as One who is ready to punish him, but as One who guides him. The hand of God signifies His power, and so David is saying that, although he be far removed from his earthly home, yet God's power leads him. That the uttermost part of the sea is conceived as being extremely distant, is shown by the phrase 'even there'. It is as though David had said, 'Even in the uttermost part of the sea, far as that be from Jerusalem, even there God's comforting power is present.'

That power or hand of God leads David as a shepherd leads his sheep or a father his child. The place is distant and David knows it not, yet God's power is leading him.

The thought is implied that wherever David is, God's hand leads him. In his own palace at Jerusalem God is with him to guide, and even in a place as distant as the farthermost part of the sea, God also guides him. He can neither escape from God nor flee from His providential care.

Again David expresses his thoughts in chiastic manner: 'Thy hand will lead me, and there will take hold of me thy right hand.' In the second member of the sentence he points out more specifically how God will lead him. The right hand of God will take hold of him so that he will neither stumble nor fall. Earlier David had pictured life as a way. It is to be expected that at home while David walks the course of life God is present with him. What is wonderful about the present thought is that even though the Psalmist is as far away as the uttermost part of the sea, God will still stretch forth His right hand to take hold of him and lead him. Even in that far away place there will be pitfalls and turnings from the way. Yet there is no need for fear, for God is present and He guides His own just as He does when they are at home.

How great these thoughts are! They distinguish the religion of the Bible from all false religion and from all false conceptions of God. The nations worship gods of their own devising; gods which they themselves have constructed in their image and according to their likeness. Yet the gods to which men bow down are unable to lead a man in the pilgrimage of life. They have no right hand with which to lead a man in his earthly life, and even if they did possess a right hand, it would be of no avail, for they themselves do not know the way that man must travel. The gods of the nations are but idols, and cannot help man. To extend the thought of the Psalmist we may declare that all religions and all philosophies and explanations of the meaning of life which are the product of mere human thinking, and so have man for their author and originator, are unable to help man. Man himself as he travels through life is in error. How then can the gods which he has made or the philosophies of life which he has constructed lead him aright along the difficult path that he must travel? Only God, who is both omniscient and omnipresent, can lead man. God has a right hand, and that right hand can guide man so that he walks in the right path that leads finally to the city of God.

Before we leave this verse we must note one point concerning its form which is quite striking. There is a remarkable contrast between THY and ME which brings to the fore both the dependence of man upon God and also the great difference between God and man. If we print the pronouns in capital letters, the contrast will be clearer. 'THY hand will lead ME, and there will seize ME THY right hand.' The distance between God and man is infinite, but even in the uttermost parts of the sea God is present to lead David wherever he must go. Wherever we are upon this earth, no matter how distant it be from our homes, there is our God strong to lead us that we fall not.

11. If I say, Surely the darkness shall cover me; even the night shall be light about me.

INASMUCH as there is no escape from God by journeying to the far corners of the universe, possibly there is another avenue of escape. Possibly the darkness can so cover David that God's eye cannot pierce it and behold him. Apparently it was the practice of some in ancient times to look upon the darkness as a kind of magical covering which could protect one from any piercing eye. David, therefore, we are sometimes told, is said to invoke a magical formula, as it were, in order to escape from God's presence. We may be sure, however, that David knew his God well enough not to do anything so foolish as to employ a magical formula.

What the Psalmist does is simply point out that the darkness, which might be thought to be so thick that no one could see through it, is nevertheless not so thick but that God can see through it. Indeed, to God, it is as though it did not exist; it is like the light. Before we consider David's words more closely, however, we must note precisely what these words are.

Does David wish to say that, inasmuch as separation by distance from God's presence has shown itself to be impossible, for that reason he has spoken? If that is his thought, we may paraphrase it somewhat as follows: 'If I could ascend to the height or descend to the depth, if I could travel with lightning-like rapidity and even go to the uttermost part of the sea, it is clear that I could not escape from the presence of God. Therefore, since I cannot escape His presence I have spoken.' That is one way of considering the opening words of this eleventh verse.

Another way, however, is to regard them as simply introducing one more hypothetical suggestion. On this interpretation the Psalmist is saying, 'If I should say', or 'Suppose I should say, etc.' Probably this latter interpretation best brings out the actual force of the Psalmist's language, but of this we cannot be sure.

David gives expression to the belief that the darkness will cover him. The verb that he uses actually means 'to bruise'. It is found in Genesis 3 : 15, where the Lord says that the Seed of the Woman will bruise the serpent's head. But how can such a word be employed of darkness? How can darkness bruise anyone? Possibly the thought is of oppressive darkness that closes in upon one and seems to overwhelm him. At any rate, two of the ancient translations of the Bible, the Septuagint and the Vulgate, have been content so to understand the word. Strange as the figure is, it may be that its actual meaning is the correct one. David then is speaking not merely of the covering of darkness, but of the fact that darkness is thick and heavy and closes in upon him. Under such conditions, when men might think that they could perform evil deeds with impunity, since they love the darkness more than the light, can there be an escape from God?

With respect to the latter clause of the verse, there are two possible interpretations. One interpretation would continue the thought introduced by the first clause. The thought of the whole verse then would be, 'And I said, Surely the darkness will cover me, and night will the light be about me.' On this interpretation the word 'night' is placed first and so made emphatic. Light for David has departed and become night. The second clause is thus made to be a parallel to the first and the whole verse is incomplete in meaning. To complete the meaning, we must await the twelfth verse.

On the other hand it is possible that the verse is complete in itself. Thus, on this view David is saying, 'And I said, Surely the darkness will cover me, yet the night will be light about me.' If this interpretation is correct, then the thought is that even though the oppression of darkness covers David, the night will be like light about him. It will no more be able to hide or obscure him from the eyes of God than the broad daylight. If this be what David means, he then goes on to explain how it is so.

Perhaps we cannot decide with any positiveness between these two positions, for a fairly strong case can be made out for each one of them. We may note, however, that in either case the meaning is essentially the same. And so it frequently is in the study of the Bible, particularly the Old Testament. There are times when the meaning of a verse is not as clear to us as we may desire. In such cases, when it seems that two interpretations are possible, we should note that they often do not differ from one another to any serious extent, and the meaning is usually essentially the same. It does not matter whether David is saying that if the darkness oppress him, the night will be as light about him, or whether he is declaring that if the darkness oppress him and the light be as night about him, then the darkness cannot hide from God, for the meaning of the two is essentially the same. In either case what is clear is the fact that God's eye is all-seeing and can penetrate even the obscuring darkness. Thick as the darkness may be, and oppressive as it may be, it cannot hide from God.

In saying that there are two possible interpretations of these words, we do not mean to suggest that the Bible is not a clear book. The Bible is a clear book, and its message of salvation is crystal clear. What we are to believe about God and what duty He requires of us is set forth in the Bible so plainly that anyone may read it and understand it. The central message of the Bible is not veiled in obscurity and darkness. It stands forth with the brightness of the noonday sun. The questions which we are now considering, however, do not affect the basic message of the Bible; these are simply questions of interpretation about details, questions which must be faced by all serious students of Scripture.

An objection, however, may be raised. Some may say that they are not interested in questions of grammar and simply would read the Bible for themselves. In answer to such an objection it must be pointed out that we cannot obtain the message of the Bible unless we first understand the language in which the Bible is written. For this reason, we must spend time seeking to understand what it is that the Holy Spirit, the Author of Scripture, wishes to say.

One thing surely is clear. David is convinced that the darkness cannot hide him from the all-seeing eye of God. The darkness to God is like the light. If one would flee from God, he needs something better than darkness to hide him.

12. Yea, the darkness hideth not from thee; but the night shineth as the day: the darkness and the light are both alike to thee.

W<small>HAT</small> is the relationship of this verse to the preceding? If we have translated verse eleven: 'And I said, Surely the darkness covers me and night is as the light about me,' we are left with a clause hanging in the air, and we must complete the clause. It would then be the task of verse twelve to complete the thought; verse twelve would be what the grammarians call an apodosis. That is, it would fill out or bring to completion the thought introduced in the eleventh verse. If, then, according to this construction, the darkness covers David and the light is as the night about him, even this darkness cannot hide from God.

On the other hand, if we have taken the eleventh verse as complete in itself, we should consider the present verse as giving an explanation why the darkness cannot obscure from God. The darkness is thick, and if anything could hide from God, it would be darkness. Men seem to think that the darkness is a sufficient covering so that in its protection they can perform evil deeds. Other men cannot see them clearly. Good as darkness is as a protection and covering, however, even darkness cannot obscure from God.

Again, David employs a picture word. 'The darkness cannot make dark from Thee.' Darkness before God cannot do what darkness is supposed to do. It cannot make dark before God. It is as though there were no darkness, for it loses its power, so that it is not able to hide or conceal anyone.

Nor does the night have any protecting or concealing power. Not only does it fail to hide David from God's all-seeing eye, but the night instead causes light to shine just as does daytime. In other words, the night acts like the day. It is the function and purpose of the night to make darkness; day's purpose, however, is to cause light to shine. Yet the night does not do what it should do; instead, the night causes light to appear. The night takes over the purpose of the day and brings forth light. Night gives out light from itself as though it were day. It acts like its opposite.

In a succinct phrase David presents the whole matter: 'Like the darkness, like the light.' This is a forceful way of saying that the darkness and the light are the same thing. No distinction is to be made between them, for neither of them can hide from God. In God's sight it is immaterial whether there be night or day, light or darkness. Neither can influence or affect God; neither can condition Him, for He depends upon neither. He is above all that He has created, and this includes both the night and the day. The light of the sun does not give Him light, and the darkness of night does not bring Him repose. He dwells in light unapproachable, and is Himself light. No earthly light or darkness are needed by Him. Thus, there fails the last means of escape from God.

13. For thou hast possessed my reins: thou hast covered me in my mother's womb.

WITH this verse we make quite a transition in the thought. Having spoken of the possibility of fleeing from God, the Psalmist now adopts the opposite course of turning in a personal manner unto God and reflecting upon the fact that God has created him. The verse begins with a 'for', and this word introduces the reason why God is all-knowing and also omnipresent, and that reason is found in the fact that God is the creator. God knows the entirety of David's life, both his outward existence and the thoughts of his heart. From this God there is no way of escape, and the reason why God possesses this knowledge and why God is everywhere present is simply that God has created all things and He has created David.

David continues addressing God, again with an emphatic THOU. To translate the verb which the Psalmist employs is not easy. It here means to acquire by creation. Possibly, despite the fact that the translation does entail some difficulties, we should best render the word 'create'. David, therefore, is saying that it is God, and only God, who has created his loins. The word rendered 'loins' means simply 'the kidneys', and these are here conceived as the seat of the emotions and will. It is a strange expression, but is found in the same sense elsewhere in the Old Testament. 'Oh let the wickedness of the wicked come to an end; but establish the just: for the righteous God trieth the hearts and reins' (Psalm 7: 9); 'Examine me, O Lord, and prove me; try my reins and my heart' (Psalm 26: 2).

To use the expression 'kidneys' seems strange. Yet by this expression David is simply referring to what may be called the seat of his pains and pleasures, of his strongest sensibilities. If God has created the reins, then God has control of David in such a way that the control reaches to the inmost part of his being.

By means of the second part of the verse David wishes to show how God has a control over his whole being. What, however, is it that the Psalmist actually says in this second part of the verse? The difficulty arises with respect to the verb. Does David say, 'Thou hast covered me'? or does he say, 'Thou hast woven me together'? The answer to this question is not easy, despite what some students of the Bible maintain. If we look at the old translations of the Bible, such as, for example, the Latin, we find that they assume that David is saying, 'Thou hast covered me.' On the other hand, the verb is capable of the translation, 'to weave', and therefore, many take it in the sense of interweave, i.e. with sinews, veins and bones. Yet if the word does refer to the act of weaving, then this is probably the only place in the Old Testament where the verb has this significance.

Although there is a difference in the force of the two

translations, nevertheless, it is not a crucial difference. Is David asserting that God has covered him in the womb of his mother, or rather is he declaring that God has woven him together in the womb of his mother? Perhaps we cannot tell, although it may be that, after all, the old traditional interpretation is correct. It does have the strength of tradition on its side, and that is not always lightly to be cast aside.

David is speaking of the embryo. When as yet he was in the womb of his mother before actual birth, he was in God's control. And this was not in some vague way, but God even then knew him intimately. God had either brought together, weaving as it were, the parts of his body, if we employ the one interpretation, so that he was wholly under God's control, or else God had covered him in the womb of the mother. From human sight he was hidden but not from the eyes of God. Even in this unborn stage, David was in God's hands.

It is one thing to speak of creation in general; it is something else to realize that God is our personal Creator. We are not the creatures of chance, merely happening in some inexplicable way to appear upon the scene of history. We are here, for God has created us, and from the first instant of our creation, even before our birth, we were wholly in His care.

Truly the doctrine of divine providence is a blessed thing. It teaches that God cares for us. And the reason why this doctrine is a blessed one is that it goes hand in hand with the doctrine of creation. Before birth, while we were yet in the womb of the mother, God watched over our ways, and the reason why He did this is that it is He that formed us. He brought the embryo into existence. From the very beginning then, we were in God's hands.

*14. I will praise thee; for I am
fearfully and wonderfully made;
marvellous are thy works:
and that my soul knoweth right well.*

D<small>AVID</small> cannot continue the development of his thought; it is too great, too vast, too all-embracing. Before such a God he does what he cannot refrain from doing. In genuine Pauline style, he breaks off in the midst of his argument, and bursts forth into thanksgiving and praise to God. 'I will praise thee', he declares. Before he can continue with the setting forth of his thought, he must turn his mind to the all-important work of praising God. Indeed, one cannot think of God and His wondrous works without bursting forth into praise. This is the reason why in so many textbooks of theology, even in the midst of their exposition of the truth, the author allows his feelings of love and praise to God to break through. It is well that such is the case. To be pitied is the man who can discourse about the greatness of God without emotion. He who knows God and loves Him cannot speak of Him without feeling. The greatness of His works of creation calls forth the adoration and praise of the human heart.

If we are not moved to praise by the contemplation of God's attributes, we may well examine our hearts whether we possess the true knowledge of God. When the devout heart begins to contemplate the greatness of God, it loses itself in wonder, love and praise.

Each word of this verse is worthy of particular note. The word 'for' introduces the second clause, but in the original Hebrew the expression contains two words. We may bring out the thought by translating 'upon (the fact) that'. What David means is that the action of his praising God rests upon the fact that God has made him. In English we might use the expression 'forasmuch as'. David indeed had a reason for praising God, and this reason lay in the fact of creation. It is not the creation as such, however, that David ponders, but the creation of himself. He is a creature of God. God has made him, he realizes, and that in a most wondrous manner.

Yet the language of the Psalmist's expression is strange. Perhaps we can best understand it if we render the Hebrew in a literal fashion. 'Forasmuch as in respect to fearful things I am distinguished.' Surely a strange statement; what does it mean? What does David wish to assert concerning himself? Perhaps we should first note his statement, 'I am distinguished.' David is referring to himself as set apart from the lower beings that God has created.

What distinguishes David is that which he calls 'fearful things'. These 'fearful things' are those things which cause fear and astonishment. They are the circumstances which surround the coming into being of David. The growth of the embryo in the mother's womb, the mysterious combination of bones and sinews – all that is involved in David's coming into being – is included in these words 'fearful things'.

How awe-inspiring is the birth of a child! In the mother's womb the strange act of conception has taken place. Life has come into existence. A growth occurs. And this embryo will come forth one day from the body of the mother and a human being will be born. Truly these are fearful things. To think upon them is to begin to realize at least to an extent the greatness of the God who can create and bring life into existence. And we should think upon these things! The very wonder of the circumstances under which life is conceived and the embryo formed should produce fear within our hearts, for we are then in the presence of the Author of Life.

Having considered the wonder of his own creation, David now proceeds to a more general contemplation. Not only is his own being wonderful, but the same may be said of all God's works. David is a master of words, and he very interestingly employs two roots which are closely related. The first of these, consisting of the letters P L H, is the root of the word which we have rendered 'I am distinguished'. The second, however, is spelled P L A, and this is the root which we translate 'wonderful'. The two words built upon these roots stand side by side. Possibly the force and significance of this may be brought out in a paraphrase. 'With respect to fearful things *I am distinguished,* yea, *wonderful* are (all) thy works.'

The words of this last clause appear to be uttered with conviction, and express the strong belief of the speaker. The works of God to which David refers are, it would seem, in this context, primarily those of creation, although it may be that the statement is more general and intended to include all of God's works, whatever they may be. In saying that these works are wonderful, the Psalmist employs a root that is generally used of miracles which the Lord has performed. It designates that which is extraordinary and filled with wonder. Hence, it is a fitting word to employ of the miracles of God to indicate that these events are set apart and distinct from ordinary events and also that they are wondrous.

All God's deeds are filled with wonder. Man cannot grasp them in the sense of comprehending them, for they are wondrous. And if all God's deeds are wondrous, particularly is this true of the creation and formation of man. This is an act that only God can perform; it is an act of wonder. All men do not realize this, but David knows it well, and he wishes to give strong attestation to this fact. 'And as for my soul,' we may render 'she knows right well'. Whatever may be true of others, David himself does know that God's deeds are wonderful. In speaking of his soul, David simply refers to himself.

How has David come to this conviction? More to the point, we might ask how this conviction has come to David? Is not the answer clear? David was a man after God's own heart. Despite the enormity of his sins, he did love the Lord and desire His glory. As a believer in the Lord David could contemplate himself and all God's works and come to the realization that they were wondrous works. Unlike the unbeliever David acknowledged that these were works of God. He did not merely dismiss them offhand with references to nature; David was a true theist. These works which aroused his fear and admiration were the works of God. Well will it be for us, too, if when we contemplate the mystery of birth, we also tremble, for we are in the presence of fearful things which God has wrought.

15. *My substance was not hid from thee, when I was made in secret, and curiously wrought in the lowest parts of the earth.*

IN CONTEMPLATING the wondrous manner in which he has been formed, David proceeds to assert that from the very beginning he was known to God. When he says 'there was not hid from thee', he means, 'thou didst assuredly see'. It is but another way of declaring that nothing can be hidden from God. In speaking of his embryo the Psalmist employs an interesting word. It actually means 'strength' and as here used refers to bones and sinews as the strength and frame of the human body. Even before his birth God saw clearly the frame of David's being.

In our modern parlance we should simply speak of the human embryo. That this is what David means is shown by the fact that he asserts that God saw his substance even while it was made in secret. To man the embryo is secret, for it is covered over by the womb of the mother. To God, however, it is in no sense secret or hidden. His eye clearly sees and He knows the embryo in its every aspect. David was made in secret, in that his embryo came into being and was formed in the womb of the mother. This wonderful fact, so little known and understood by man, is clearly understood and known to God. 'It is he that hath made us, and not we ourselves.' The origin of our being is in His hands. Herein is another evidence of His omniscience and mighty power.

David adds to what he has just said, in that he declares, 'I was curiously wrought in the lower parts of the earth.' Actually he speaks of being embroidered. It is a strange and bold word, but it refers to the mysterious manner in which the bones and sinews of the human body are knit together. Possibly the emphasis falls upon the variegated colouring as shown by the veins of the body.

What, however, is the meaning of the strange expression, 'in the lowest parts of the earth'? In what sense can it be said that man was 'embroidered' or 'fashioned' in the lowest parts of the earth? The phrase obviously stands in parallelism to 'in secret'. David was formed in secret and in the depths of the earth. If, therefore, the phrase 'in secret' refers to the womb of the mother, it would seem also that 'the depths of the earth' is a figurative expression for the same thing. Perhaps there is an allusion here to the fact that man was formed of the dust of the ground, and the suggestion that the mother's body is dust. Elihu says, for example, 'Behold, I am according to thy wish in God's stead; I also am formed out of the clay' (Job 33 : 6). The mother's womb is of the earth, and so in speaking of being formed of clay, Elihu means that he has come from the mother's womb.

Here the figure simply serves to emphasize that the womb of the mother is a place of darkness wherein the body of man is formed. We are being told by some modern students of the Bible that in this phrase there is to be found a reflection upon ancient mythology. Here, they say, the earth is pictured as the mother of all living things. These ancient myths, so the argument goes, were not original with Israel, but were taken over from her Canaanitish neighbours and were applied by the Israelites to their own god. According to this supposed myth man apparently arose in the deep depths of the dark earth. Now, however, the conception has appeared in Israel that the God of Israel is present and beholds the birth of man in the heart of the earth. This myth, it is suggested, was earlier than the account in Genesis 2: 7, where we are told that the Lord Himself formed man.

What shall we say to this idea of an ancient myth being reflected here in the Psalm? There is only one thing to say about it, and that is that there is not one particle of evidence that such a myth was ever accepted in Israel. Whether other nations really believed that man was created in the heart or depth of the earth or not, we do not know. One thing we do know – the Israelites never accepted any such belief, and there is not a word in the Bible to support such a belief. What the Israelites believed about the creation of man is recorded in the first two chapters of the Bible, and if there are any chapters in the Bible that are free from myth, those are the chapters.

16. Thine eyes did see my substance,
yet being unperfect; and in thy book
all my members were written,
which in continuance were fashioned,
when as yet there was none of them.

*H*ERE, indeed, is a difficult verse. The words 'my substance, yet being unperfect', represent just one word in the original Hebrew. This word is placed first in the sentence for emphasis' sake. We pronounce it *golmi*. The word is derived from a verb which means to roll or to roll up, and so would seem to refer to something rolled together. Hence it is usually applied to the human foetus. Objection has been raised against this interpretation, for it is asserted that to mention the embryo here does not comport well with the remainder of the chapter. It has also been suggested that the idea present is that of an embryo rolled into the shape of an egg, but that seems to read too much into the word. We cannot deny that the verse is difficult, and the precise force of *golmi* is certainly difficult also. Nevertheless, it would seem that there is here a reference to the embryo, although exactly how the embryo is to be conceived is a question that we must leave open.

At any rate, the Psalmist continues his prayer to God, declaring that God's eyes have seen his embryo. Throughout the Psalm we have been thinking of God as one who looked down upon the children of men. Now, there is a specific reference to God's eyes. Perhaps the reference points to the difference between God's eyes and those of men. Men's eyes cannot behold the mysterious and strange process of the development of the embryo, for it is hidden to them. To God, however, the body of the mother is no covering, and God's eyes penetrate through the body, so that from Him nothing can be hidden.

The Psalmist now asserts that upon God's book all of 'them' are written down. We may ask, 'All of what?' The King James Version reads, 'all my members were written', but we should notice that the words 'my members' are in italics, and this means that they are not found in the original Hebrew. They have simply been inserted into the English translation for the purpose of making it more readable and understandable. We, however, are dealing with the rugged Hebrew language, and in the Hebrew we have a problem. What is written down in God's book?

One way out of the difficulty is to translate the word *golmi* not as embryo, but as bundle, and to refer it to the days of David's life. We would then have the following thought: 'Thine eyes did see the bundle of my life, and upon thy book all these days are written.' This is certainly one possibility for dealing with a difficult problem. Whether it is the correct possibility or not is another question.

Another way and one which we think has more to commend it is to construe 'all of them' with the word 'days' which follows. We then get this sense, 'Thine eyes did see my embryo, and in thy book all of them, namely, the days, are written down.' This is possible, and in the light of the various considerations involved, is probably the best way to bring out the thought of this very difficult verse.

What is meant, we may well ask, when the Psalmist asserts that all the days are written upon God's book? It has been said that the expression 'the book of the Lord' is somewhat analogous to the Babylonian tablets of destiny, on which the destinies of men were written. Possibly there is a formal similarity, but the similarity ceases at that point. The conception of a book of God is found elsewhere in the Old Testament. Thus, the Psalmist says, 'Thou tellest my wanderings: put thou my tears into thy bottle: are they not in thy book?' (Psalm 56: 8); 'Let them be blotted out of the book of the living, and not be written with the righteous' (Psalm 69: 28); 'Yet now, if thou wilt forgive their sin—; and if not, blot me, I pray thee, out of thy book which thou hast written; and the Lord said unto Moses, Whosoever hath sinned against me, him will I blot out of my book' (Exodus 32: 32, 33).

God has a book, and in this book he writes the names of his people. In the New Testament this book is referred to as the Lamb's book of life, and only those will enter the heavenly city whose names are written therein. In the Psalm, however, the conception or at least the emphasis is a bit different. The thought here is that the entirety of the Psalmist's being, even including the days of his life, are inscribed in the book that belongs to God.

By the days of his life the Psalmist has in mind all the vicissitudes that he must experience. All of his life, each individual day with all that that day will bring, is written down by God in His own book.

Furthermore, it is stated that these days of the Psalmist's life have been formed before there were any of them. If we translate the Hebrew literally, we may notice what an expressive thought is here given. 'Days were formed, and there (was) not one among them.' Expressive as is this thought, it is nevertheless difficult and requires careful consideration. What actually is the Psalmist saying? If we understand his language aright, he is saying that the days of his life were actually formed before even one of them had come into existence. All his life, the details of each day, had been written down in the book of God, before any of these days had actually occurred.

The Psalmist has here reached a peak in his exaltation of the all-knowing and all-powerful God. Not only does God know all things, but God has also foreordained all things. In other words, the Psalmist has brought us head on with the doctrine of predestination. His life he regards not as a chance happening, but as a life already planned by God even before he himself was born. All the days that David would live and all the events of each day had been written down in God's book before David himself had come into existence.

Although the language of the verse is difficult, nevertheless, the thought is perfectly clear, and like the Psalms generally, it gives all glory to God. No wonder that there are those who would like to avoid coming head on with the clear-cut teaching of this verse. We are told, for example, that there is no theoretical, speculative doctrine of predestination here. True enough, the Psalmist does not present the doctrine in a carefully formulated manner, but the doctrine is here. Then again we, are told that what is presented here does not stand in basic conflict with human freedom. True, it does not conflict with the fact of human responsibility, but we fear that such statements as the two just given are made for the purpose of obscuring the clear-cut teaching of the passage.

When all is said and done the fact remains that the doctrine of predestination is taught in this verse, and there is no legitimate way of removing it. David's life is not determined by David; he is not the master of his fate nor the captain of his soul, nor, for that matter, is any man. Before David appeared upon this earth, the days of his life had been determined by God Himself. Indeed, all that occurs has been foreordained of God. God has a plan and hence there are no surprises for Him. He knows what the future will bring forth, for He Himself has determined that future. David was to live a life that had been pre-determined for him.

David does not rebel at this thought and neither should we. The contemplation of this profound doctrine leads him to an utterance of the preciousness of God's thoughts. He is willing that it should be as set forth here. He is content that God has determined in advance his life, predestined the course of events for him. As a devout believer in the Lord he knows that whatever God does is right.

Nevertheless, objections to the Scriptural teaching are constantly raised. Does not this present a mechanistic view of the universe? it is asked. Does not this take away from the freedom of the creature? Before we even consider such objections, we must remember that our purpose is not to harmonize the teaching of the Bible with our limited and finite reason. When we seek to bring the revealed word of God down to the level of our finite reason, we very often do violence to the Scriptures. There are teachings in the Bible which to our full satisfaction we cannot understand nor even comprehend. We are not for that reason at liberty to reject these teachings. The important thing for us at this point is to ascertain whether the Bible actually does teach this doctrine of predestination, and having ascertained that it does, to accept the doctrine with humble and believing and even rejoicing hearts.

At the same time we may confidently assert that the fact of divine predestination does not in any sense do violence to our human responsibility. The Bible is filled with commands addressed to us setting forth what God requires of us. It is not necessary for us to harmonize these commands with the Scriptural emphasis upon divine sovereignty as manifested in the foreordination of whatsoever comes to pass. We know that the very fact that God has proclaimed both His sovereignty and also the responsibility of the creature is sufficient warrant for us to believe in both. In God they find their harmony, and that is sufficient for the believer. We can trust God and leave the question of harmonization to Him. David, apparently, was willing to do just that.

There is something else that we can do. In the light of this profound teaching of the Bible we can bow in devout adoration before our great God. What a wonderful thing it is to know that the very days of our lives have been written down in His book even before these days come into existence! Life is filled with difficulty. About us the world seems to be in turmoil. We see men in desperation and agony, for they know not the meaning of life. Is life, after all, just a chaos? Is it a tale 'told by an idiot, full of sound and fury, signifying nothing'? We know better; we know that our days are in God's hands. We can sing with the hymn writer,

'Whate'er my God ordains is right;
Here shall my stand be taken;
Though sorrow, need, or death be mine,
Yet am I not forsaken;
My Father's care is round me there:
He holds me that I shall not fall,
And so to Him I leave it all.'

17. How precious also are thy thoughts unto me, O God! how great is the sum of them!

WHAT effect does such divine scrutiny and knowledge of David's being and ways have upon the Psalmist? He calls attention to himself in order that he may state what his own reaction is. And the reaction is not surprising. David does not exhibit resentment at God's close scrutiny of himself; instead he marvels at the wonder of the incomprehensible thoughts of his great God. The first words of the verse as they are found in the Hebrew may be rendered 'and to me'. The thought is: 'therefore, as respects me'. In the light of the grandeur of God's thoughts David is willing to show what consequence applies to himself. He directs our thought to himself, therefore, not in any sense to praise himself, but rather to exhibit how he reacts to the divine scrutiny and knowledge of which he has been speaking.

This is well, for the Psalm is, after all, a prayer. It is not a technical statement of the truths of God's omniscience and omnipotence, but rather a presentation of these truths with respect to David himself. And what is said here concerning David should also apply to all who like David love and reverence the Lord as their God. The Psalm thus exhibits a practical purpose; it is designed to promote godliness among those who are God's own, and nothing can produce godliness more effectively than the contemplation of the attributes of the majestic God of whom this Psalm speaks.

David bursts forth in an ejaculation. This is not the first time in the Psalter that David has done this. Elsewhere he also exclaims over the works and thoughts of God: 'O Lord, how great are thy works! and thy thoughts are very deep' (Psalm 92: 5). God's lovingkindness also calls forth his admiration: 'How excellent is thy lovingkindness, O God! therefore the children of men put their trust under the shadow of thy wings' (Psalm 36: 7). This is as it should be. He who can study and contemplate the deep truths of God and remain cold and passive reflects a strange attitude. When we meditate upon these profound facts which the Scripture reveals, should not we be deeply moved? Our words are not adequate to express the feelings of emotion that should arise within us as we come face to face with the great truths revealed in the sacred Scriptures. He who can remain unmoved by these truths and consider them merely as so many objects of study must indeed have a cold heart. David was not such a one, nor should we be. David could not but cry out in wonder for he was overwhelmed by the enormity of the truth which he was pondering.

'How precious are thy thoughts,' he exclaims. The word basically means 'to be heavy', and then comes to have the significance, 'to be valuable'. Some interpreters of the Bible believe that David is here speaking of difficulty in understanding God's thoughts. This interpretation is very old; it was advanced by the Jewish rabbi, Kimchi, and in this he has been followed by a number of the better German expositors. Nevertheless, this does not seem to be the correct meaning. David is not expressing astonishment at the difficulty of understanding or grasping the thoughts of God; what David is expressing is his own reaction to these thoughts. He does not resent them, but rather regards them as precious. They are his own cherished possession. To think them and to meditate upon them is his chief delight.

The thoughts of God of which David speaks are those which God has concerning David, thoughts which are constantly directed to him and which have embraced and do embrace him in the entirety of his life. These thoughts which have originated with God reveal how great God is. They show that He is truly omniscient, omnipresent and omnipotent.

In addressing God, David is not content to employ the ordinary word for God. Instead of that, he uses a word (EL) which stresses the distinction between God and man. The ordinary word (ELOHIM) may at times be employed of those that are less than God. Not so the word EL. This word is unique. David is approaching His Creator, One who is infinitely exalted above himself. He will not use any word that might possibly lead to misunderstanding. He dares now to address God only with the word EL. Thus he brings out the fact that he is but a creature speaking to the One who is the true God.

The second half of the verse also contains an exclamation, 'How great is the sum of them!' It is difficult to bring out in English the precise force of the Hebrew. The word 'great' may be rendered 'strong' and refers to the number of God's thoughts. It probably also includes reflection upon the power and greatness of the thoughts themselves. David speaks of the sum of these thoughts, and the actual Hebrew word is the normal word for 'head'. It may be well if we simply translate literally, 'How has become strong the head of them!' It would seem that David is uttering his surprise at the power of the thoughts of God. The total impact which they make upon him is that of strength. If this is so, it would appear that he is thinking of more than the number of God's thoughts. Surely these thoughts, at least to David, are numberless, but it is not that alone which overwhelms him. It is the strength which the full force of the thoughts makes that staggers him.

18. If I should count them, they are more in number than the sand: when I awake, I am still with thee.

THE thoughts of God are so many that David cannot possibly count them. Actually, the Psalmist does not use a conditional sentence, 'If I should count them'. What he says is far stronger. 'I will count them', he says, and then, as though to show the impossibility of his determination, adds, 'they are more in number than sand'. In the Scriptures sand is an example of what cannot be counted. The promise to Abraham, for example, was '. . . I will multiply thy seed as the stars of the heaven, and as the sand which is upon the sea shore . . .' (Genesis 22: 17). Here the reference to sand is emphatic and is placed first. 'From sand they would be more.' If the thoughts of God are more numerous than the sand, then they must be numerous indeed.

These thoughts of God which arouse the adoring wonder of David are before him night and day. There is no escape from them. According to some David has been contemplating the divine thoughts seeking to count them and in so doing has become wearied and fallen asleep. When he awakes refreshed from this sleep he makes the discovery that he is still with God, and God's thoughts are still before him.

It is, however, very questionable whether this is the meaning of the verse. There is nothing here to suggest that David simply counted the thoughts of God, one by one, as we supposedly count sheep when we want to fall asleep, and that in this counting he became tired out and succumbed to slumber. Not at all. First of all, the act of counting the thoughts of God means far more than listing these thoughts and numbering them one, two, three, and so on. In counting the thoughts of God David was not merely seeking to find out how many thoughts God had, but rather was meditating upon these thoughts. It is true that the verse does stress the quantitative aspect of the matter, the number of God's thoughts in comparison with the sand, but as David proceeds to count or number these thoughts he is thinking upon them. It is not only the number but also the greatness of the thoughts which impresses him.

Night does not exclude David from the thoughts which God has of him. When the morning comes he is still with God. It is important to note the word 'still', for it implies that the night had not separated David from God. To say that when he awakes he is still with God is to imply that he has been with God right along throughout the night. In fact, the purpose of the verse is to show that even the night does not separate from God. During the night as well as in the morning he is still with God. 'I awake,' says the Psalmist, 'and still am I with thee.'

One of the advantages of a knowledge of Hebrew is that it enables one to appreciate the assonances (similarities of sound) which characterize the language. And here at the close of the verse there is such an assonance. The words may be transliterated. ODEE IMMAHK. Our transliteration is not entirely satisfactory. Both of the words begin with the same consonant; one concludes with a suffix of the first person (ME), and the other with the suffix of the second person (THEE). We may render, 'And still am *I* with *THEE*'. It is a forceful way of bringing together David and God.

19. *Surely thou wilt slay the wicked, O, God: depart from me therefore, ye bloody men.*

*F*ROM the contemplation of the thoughts of God David turns abruptly to the consideration of the fact that there are enemies of this God. This must not be! These enemies have no right to existence, for if they triumph, God is not what David has considered Him to be. Hence, the Psalmist utters his conviction and assurance that God will slay the wicked.

Actually David is uttering a wish, but the form of his language creates some difficulties. In form the words constitute a condition: 'if thou wilt slay the wicked'. Then we expect to add a conclusion such as, 'then I shall praise thee'. Perhaps we can best bring out the thought in English if we translate, 'Oh! that thou wouldst slay the wicked!' The expression is reminiscent of the book of Job. For one thing, the verb translated 'slay' occurs only in this Psalm and in the book of Job. Then again, the word for God, ELOAH, is found more frequently in Job than anywhere else in the Old Testament.

Why, however, does David give utterance to such an expression? According to a modern interpretation the Psalmist had fallen into persecution. The evil ones had accused him falsely and sought after his life. In his own enemies, therefore, he also recognizes the enemies of the Lord. Hence, he approaches God to try him and prove him, and, according to verse one, this examination has already taken place. Chronologically, therefore, we are told, verses 19–24 belong before verses 1–18. What determines the form of the Psalm, however, it is said, is not chronology and biography but the praise of God which appears at the beginning of the Psalm.

Others have thought that the concluding verses of the Psalm, namely verses 19–24, are independent and should be divorced from the first eighteen verses. The last verse of the Psalm, however, clearly reflects upon the first verse. There is also a development of thought in the Psalm which shows that it is a unity, and that it is not to be divided into two parts.

It has been held that the Psalm belongs to a type of poetry known as Lamentation. It has also been held that the Psalm basically belongs to the type known as 'hymn' but that the Psalmist goes far beyond the ordinary form of such hymns. The Psalm has been assigned to the category of 'Prayers of the Accused', and also considered as a preparation for the divine declaration of judgment which took place in the frame of the religious cult. Indeed, it has even been held that the idea of judgment is rooted in the tradition of the cult.

From these various explanations we may safely turn away. We are living in a day when a tremendous amount of study has been devoted to the Psalms. Much of this study centres about the question, what was the situation in life which gave rise to the Psalms? Attention is accordingly paid to the classification into which each Psalm is supposed to fit. Much of this study is really of little profit, although much of it also is worth while. One who reads modern commentaries on the Psalms must read with caution and discernment. We may appreciate the good in much of this modern study, but on the whole, we do not feel that it has led to a profound understanding of the Psalms.

From these modern studies of the Psalms we may turn away and ask again why it is that David utters this strong wish for the destruction of his enemies. The answer to this question, we believe, is not too difficult to find.

The Psalmist has just come face to face with the reality of God. He has been spending his time engaged in the contemplation of God's infinite attributes. The thought of God's omniscience has led him to consider God's omnipresence. Then he has turned to reflection upon the almighty power of God in particular as that power was manifested in his own creation and formation. Such a God is the true God and deserves the complete and wholehearted love and devotion of all. Yet there are those who oppose this God and, were it possible, would seek to frustrate His purposes. Such people must not succeed! Either they must change their ways and turn to God or they must perish. There can be no other course. The enemies of God must be destroyed; else they will destroy the work of God.

David realizes this fact, and consequently cries out for the destruction of the wicked. He does not intend to kill the wicked himself, but leaves that to God. God, inasmuch as He is what He is, cannot allow the wicked to continue. If He does permit them to continue with their wicked opposition and enmity to Him, He is showing that He truly does not hate sin. He must act in order that His omnipotence and righteousness may be seen by all, and that they may triumph.

Before we proceed to condemn David for this prayer, it is well to note that we ourselves pray for the same thing, whenever we pray the words of the Lord's Prayer, 'Thy kingdom come, thy will be done'. When we pray that the kingdom of God should come, we are at the same time praying that the kingdom of Satan should be destroyed. And when we pray that the kingdom of Satan be destroyed, we are asking for the destruction of all those who go to make up that kingdom. If God's kingdom is to come, then all that stands in the way of that kingdom must be taken out of the way. Those men, in other words, who oppose the work of God are doing a heinous thing; they must be put out of the way. They would destroy God, were that possible. This great God whose knowledge has caused David to exclaim in wonder, is a God whom they hate. It would seem inconceivable that men should hate God, but hate Him they do. They are His enemies, and they are violent in their hatred towards Him. Surely, He will not permit them to continue their evil work. He will slay them.

David proceeds to characterize the wicked as men of blood, and by this expression is identifying them as violent men. They are men who have slain innocent blood, murderers or murderous men. In the taking of a life they have destroyed the image of God, for man is created in God's image. This God whom David adores is a God whom the wicked despise. Inasmuch as they are what they are David will have no part with them. Hence he addresses them with a command, 'Turn aside from me.' God's enemies have also become enemies of the Psalmist.

20. For they speak against thee wickedly, and thine enemies take thy name in vain.

I⊤ IS possible to translate the introductory words of this verse, 'who speak against thee wickedly'. At any rate the statement is here made that the wicked, the men of blood, speak wickedly against God. They speak of God or in some sense use His Name for the accomplishment of wicked purposes. To these wicked men God means nothing, and they are willing to use even his holy name in order that they may attain unto their own evil ends.

As though in conscious disobedience of the Ten Commandments, these wicked ones also take God's Name in vain. The reflection of the language upon the Ten Commandments is clear, but it is striking that no object of the verb is present. 'They take for vain', so we may render the words, and those who do this are the enemies of God. Perhaps this latter phrase is intended as an explanation of the former one. The sinful action of the wicked is a violation of the third commandment.

David has just contemplated the greatness of God. This God is not a creation of man, but the Creator who in all of His attributes is infinite, eternal and unchange-

able. David has been filled with awe. How great and
infinite is the Name of God! Yet wicked men treat this
Name with disdain. It is this that David cannot abide.
Such men are his enemies, for they are God's enemies
also.

21. *Do not I hate them, O Lord, that hate thee? and am not I grieved with those that rise up against thee?*

WHAT a strange verse and one so often misunderstood! How often men have turned against the utterances herein expressed and condemned them as signs of a low morality! How 'righteous' men have become, asserting vigorously that they themselves do not want to hate anyone, and that they will not sink to the level of feeling expressed in this verse! The idea of hating one's enemies is said to be barbarous and wholly contrary to the doctrine of love taught by Jesus Christ. What we have in the Psalm, men sometimes assert, is ethics of a sub-Christian level. We have advanced beyond this, and want none of it. The Hebrews, apparently, knew no better, but we now have the teaching of Jesus, and we have learned not to hate our enemies. We have Jesus, and we do not need the Psalm.

Expressions such as these are heard all too often. Before we proceed to comment upon them, there is one point that needs to be stressed. Modern man is in no position to condemn the teaching of this Psalm. He has not attained to a level of ethics from which he may look down with disdain upon the teaching of Psalm 139. It is simply not true that modern man has learned not to hate his enemies. He may pay lip service to the doctrine of loving one's enemies, but the actual fact is that, despite the so-called progress of civilization, modern men hate their enemies and even those who are not their enemies just as much as men of a former day. The human heart today all too often is filled with envy, jealousy and bitterness, even when there is no excuse for such things. Men do not love one another. They know what they ought to do, but they do not do it. And often, it would seem, those who proclaim most strongly that they are above the 'low ethics' of the Psalm are the ones who speak with bitterness and hatred of other people. The 'do-gooders' of this world, as they are sometimes called, are not at all above misrepresentation and mental persecution. They have the same faults and failures as the remainder of mankind. It is well then to remember that today, just as much as in any past day, men hate their enemies and, all too often, even their friends. Whatever else may be said about the modern age in which we live, it has not advanced to such a point that it can look down upon the teaching of Psalm 139.

A more profound consideration, however, arises. Have those who condemn out of hand what they believe to be the teaching of this Psalm really understood the Psalm? Is David sinking to a sub-Christian standard of ethics? Is he giving vent to hatred toward those whom he personally dislikes? Is he speaking from motives that are impure and unworthy? It would have been well if those who so readily condemn the Psalm would take the trouble to find out what the Psalm actually teaches before they pour out the vials of their scorn upon it.

Indeed, herein is a lesson for all those who study the Bible. When we hear criticisms raised against this or that point in the Bible, the best thing to do is to turn to the Bible and to discover what it actually says. It is not always easy to do this, but it is always profitable. When we have learned what the Bible says upon a particular matter, the objection thereto will often disappear. Much criticism of the Bible is based upon ignorance of its contents, and when this ignorance is dispelled, and the Bible is allowed to say what it actually does say, the difficulty vanishes. And so it is in the present case. Before we look more closely at the verse, we can assert at the outset that David is not giving vent to personal feelings of hatred against those who may be his personal enemies. David was a magnanimous man, and despite his great sinfulness and many shortcomings, showed that he was a man willing to forgive. He did not harbour grudges. What we read in this verse is not an expression of personal vindictiveness.

In the first place we may note that David appeals to God to corroborate his assertion that he hates those who hate God. Were there anything unworthy in David's hatred, he could not and would not appeal to God for corroboration. When a man engages in sinful action or entertains sinful thoughts, he does not go to God to support him, unless he himself is so deceived that he thinks that even in sinning he is doing God's will. It is true that some men may be so deceived that in doing wrong they think they are pleasing God. Can that be true of David?

The answer to that question is not difficult to determine. David's whole soul is overcome with a loathing against wickedness. He has just been contemplating the attributes of the great God whom he serves and his soul has been bowed down in deepest awe and reverence. When a man is thus in the presence of God, it is difficult for him to look with favour upon sin. It is this very fact of the majesty of God which causes David to realize that he must oppose those who are God's enemies. If we say that David's utterances in this verse betray a low ethical standard, what we are really saying is that the contemplation of the majesty of God leads one to actions that are ethically low. There is no escape from this conclusion, for it is out of the contemplation of God Himself that the expressions of this verse flow. We cannot say that David was deceived into thinking that he was doing right when he actually was doing wrong. Everything in the Psalm speaks against such a thought. It is an impossible interpretation. And its impossibility is further shown in that David appeals to God to search his heart and to know even his inmost thoughts. If there is any wicked way in David, he wants it removed, for he desires that God lead him in the way everlasting. Men who are sinning are not concerned that God should search their inmost thoughts and try their hearts. We cannot be satisfied with such an interpretation of this verse.

Is there not, however, another possibility? May it not be after all that the appeal to God is without meaning? Was not the God of David a tribal God, the God of the Hebrews? At this stage in their religious development, would the Israelites have had an exalted conception of Him? Had they yet learned that He was Himself of an ethical nature? Was He not bound up with the fortunes of Israel? In answer to this argument we would say that the whole Psalm speaks against it. The One to whom David here prays is no local tribal deity but the almighty Creator of heaven and earth. No higher conceptions of God have appeared anywhere than those which are found in this Psalm. Indeed, it is that very fact that has led some men to think that the Psalm was too 'advanced' for David's time. The God to whom David here prays is the same God that appears in the latter chapters of the prophecy of Isaiah, and also in the pages of the New Testament.

Of course, had David been left to his own devices and not been the recipient of special revelation, we have no way of knowing what kind of an idea of God he might have had. David was a sinful man; he was, to say the least, guilty of theft, of adultery, of responsibility for murder and for deception. Had he not heard the voice of the living God, we do not know what his ideas of God would have been. No doubt they would have been upon a level with those of the men of his time. What we have in this Psalm, however, are not simply David's ideas of God. What we have here are the heartfelt expressions of a man who knew the one living and true God and who had been the recipient of Divine revelation. We cannot then consider seriously the objection that the God of David's day was a local deity.

The Psalm therefore stands before us, and we must ask in all seriousness what it means. Attempts to deprive the language of its meaning have not proved to be satisfactory. Let us then examine more closely the expressions of this verse. The verse is a question addressed to God, and we may translate it in a word for word fashion as follows, 'Is it not that thy haters, O Lord! I hate, and against those who rise up against thee do I feel loathing?' The question is almost equivalent to saying, 'Behold!' It certifies the truthfulness of what the Psalmist is saying. David wants men to know that he does actually hate God's enemies.

These enemies are mentioned first and so placed in a position of emphasis. They are the objects of David's hatred, and they are described by the words, 'those who hate thee'. What shall be said about this hatred of the enemies of God? Is it, like David's hatred, a thing to be commended? Obviously it is not. It springs from a heart that is depraved and fallen into an estate of sin, a heart from which evil flows. This is a hatred clothed in evil and in a desire to banish God from one's thoughts. It is the God of the Bible that stands in the way of the designs of fallen man. Without God he thinks he can solve the problems of this life; he can do all that he will, but God keeps getting in the way. He therefore would suppress the knowledge of God and keep Him from all his thoughts. With religion as such he can afford to be quite tolerant. He is willing for every man to go to the church of his own choice, as long as God does not come into the picture. The wicked hate God, and would destroy Him were that possible. Those who hate God, no matter how moral their lives may appear, are wicked men. They have set themselves against Him, and their hatred of Him is an emotion in which the evil is loved and the good hated.

In speaking to God, David reverts to the word with

which he had begun the Psalm. He addresses God again as 'Lord', and thereby shows his own close dependence upon his God. This Lord is the One who brought the Israelites out of the bondage of Egypt and who had chosen them to be His people. His great electing love had brought the nation into being, indeed; it was His electing love that had called David himself from the darkness of sin into the light of salvation. It is to God, the covenant God, that he therefore appeals. This is David's own God whom wicked men hate.

Then comes the verb, and this verb possesses different connotations. We may render, 'do I not hate', or 'should I not hate' or 'must I not hate'. David knows that there can be but one reaction to such men. He must hate them. It is clear, however, from the context itself, that when David thus expresses himself, he is employing the word 'hate' in a sense different from that which applied to wicked men. Wicked men hated God, and their hatred was an evil emotion. David hated, but his hatred was like God's hatred; it proceeded from no evil emotion, but rather from the earnest and thoroughly sincere desire that the purposes of God must stand and that wickedness must perish. Had David not hated, he would have desired the success of evil and the downfall of God Himself. It is well to keep this thought in mind when we consider the nature of David's hatred.

Indeed, this point needs to be stressed. Before we assume that there was something unworthy in David's attitude, we must note precisely what that attitude was. Anything less than pure hatred of the enemies of God is an acknowledging that God is not what He should be. It is an agreeing with the position that God and His purposes need not stand. If those purposes are fulfilled in part but not entirely, then one need not hate God's enemies.

God and His enemies are arrayed in earnest combat. God's purposes of salvation must be carried through. Indeed, all His holy counsel must come to pass. Should it fail of accomplishment even in the least detail, then God will be seen to be something less than the God He claims to be. If, therefore, one desires God's purposes to be fulfilled, and so to see His holy Name exalted, he will turn wholeheartedly and absolutely against all who stand in the way of God and would, were that possible, tear Him from His throne. One must either hate the enemies of God and count them as his own enemies or else he must acknowledge that he does not desire the purposes of God to come to pass and that he does not wish God to receive the glory that is His due. One cannot be wholly devoted to God unless he hates God's enemies. Martin Luther was entirely on scriptural ground when he wrote:

> Lord, keep us steadfast in Thy Word.
> Curb those who fain by craft and sword
> Would wrest the kingdom from Thy Son
> And set at nought all He hath done.

We, too, must hate God's enemies. This we will do, however, not by personal vindictiveness, nor by malice and envy. Rather through the diligent use of the means of grace and the determined purpose of living for the glory of God and enjoying Him for ever, we will show the hatred that God requires. It has well been said that Satan fears when he sees the weakest saint upon his knees. And so it is, if we are to speak of the practical application of this truth. Let us go to Jesus in true devotion, meditate upon and study His word, and live as those whom He has redeemed with His precious blood.

In the parallel expression the Psalmist speaks of those who rise up against or assail God. Against such the Psalmist feels a loathing. These expressions we must understand in the same manner as those concerning the hatred of God's enemies. They are strong words to indicate that the believer in God must be separate from those who hate God.

At this point a misunderstanding is likely to arise. How, it may be asked, can we win other men to Christ, if we stay away from them, hating and loathing them? Those, however, who ask this question, show by the very asking thereof that they have not properly understood the meaning of the Psalm. David's hatred and loathing are not necessarily directed against particular individuals. Rather, this hatred and loathing must be shown in a positive manner. It is by serving and loving God and keeping His commandments that we are manifesting our hatred of the wicked. This may at times bring us into conflict with those who oppose God, but our dealing with them as individuals must always be in love, even where we are called upon to oppose them. By opposing them in love we are showing that we hate. Of course, we are in no position to pass an infallible judgment upon what individuals are God's and what individuals are His enemies. All we can do is to oppose evil wherever we find it, and to deal in love with those individuals who are doing wrong and apparently opposing God.

There is an example which may make the matter clear. A modernist probably never will understand why the conservative opposes him. Is not the modernist desirous of doing good? Should he not be commended for what he is doing? He who believes the Bible, however, knows that the modernist, whatever his intentions may be, is in actual fact hurting the work of Christ. Instead of exalting Jesus Christ as the only Redeemer of lost sinners, the modernist minimizes sin and assures man that he can save himself, if there is any saving work to be performed. This is a perversion of the Gospel and a dishonouring of God.

The conservative must oppose the modernist. He must do it, however, in love. He may do it forcefully and strongly and he must do it clearly. He must, however, do it in love. He has no right to stoop to abuse, or in any other way to do evil in order that good may come. It is through speaking the truth in love, thus exhibiting an earnest concern for the truth of God, that God uses him and makes the truth known. Thus, in earnestly contending for the faith, the Christian is hating the enemies of God. It may sound paradoxical, but the deeper our love to God, the greater will be our hatred of His enemies.

In the light of these considerations, it will be seen how far short of the mark is that interpretation which claims that this Psalm has not gone beyond the limits of the Old Testament. According to this interpretation it would have been more in keeping with the awe due to God if the Psalmist had realized that in the enigma which divine inscrutability supposedly raises, the wicked were also included. The Psalmist should have stopped at this point, so it is held, and simply have remained content with the truth that God's thoughts are not man's. Or, he should have realized that the fact that God permits His enemies to remain alive points to God's forbearance and compassion and that just as God's greatness transcends all human standards so also does His goodness. This divine compassion was exhibited by Jesus upon the cross. The Psalmist, however, is not able to follow it, for, we are told, he is under the influence of the cultic ideology of his time.

This interpretation is, of course, based upon the principles of form-criticism so much in vogue today. That it is not a satisfactory interpretation should be obvious. It completely misunderstands what the Psalmist is here saying. The principle that one must hate the enemies of God, as we have sought to indicate above, is not incompatible with the love of God manifested toward sinners, nor with His sincere and earnest offer of the Gospel of redemption to all men everywhere.

22. I hate them with perfect hatred: I count them mine enemies.

DAVID does not at all modify or tone down his statement. Rather, he seeks to indicate what the nature of his hatred is. 'With completeness of hatred I hate them', he declares. The first word refers to the end or extremity, so that David is saying in effect that he hates them as far as it is possible for him to do so. To the very end or completeness of hatred, he has hated them. The first word is used as an adjective, so that we might render, 'with complete hatred have I hated them'. A partial hatred would be no hatred at all; it would be tantamount to saying that David truly did not care for God and His purposes. He who only partly hates the enemies of God is one who completely hates God and is opposed to Him. Such a one David would not be. His devotion is extreme.

Perhaps a word of caution is needed here. We are living in a day when men speak of extremism as necessarily an evil thing. Yet extremism in the service of God is required. We are to love God, not in some partial fashion, but with all the heart, soul and mind. Our entire being must be consecrated to Him, and all our energies and efforts devoted to the service of our God. It is this which

David possesses. His hatred toward God's enemies is no lukewarm or middle-of-the-road hatred. Rather, with a completeness of hatred does he hate God's enemies.

'Enemies they have become to me.' Here David injects himself into the picture. God's enemies are also his enemies. This is tantamount to saying that whatever God loves David will love and whatever God hates David will hate. Of course, we must be cautious that we do not use a verse such as this as an excuse for any wrong attitudes on our part. If we hate, we must be sure that God also hates the same object. We cannot choose our objects for hatred on our own. We learn what to hate from God and from Him alone. And this we learn through the constant, deep study of His revealed Word, the Bible. Unless we walk with God, depending upon Him for all things, our hatred will be the wrong kind of hatred, and the wrong kind of hatred is sin.

23. *Search me, O God, and know my heart: try me, and know my thoughts:*

*D*AVID now reverts to the thought of the first verse. There he had said that God had searched him. Now he desires God to search him. There, the statement led to the consideration of what it was for God to search David and know him. Now, having contemplated the greatness of the ineffable God and the mystery of His attributes, he bows, as it were, in humble acknowledgment and submission and beseeches God to search him. Indeed, he so commands God. It is an acquiescence in all that has gone before. God is great in all His works and ways and David would have it so. That God knows him in the inmost depths of his being does not lead David to rebel but to praise. David rejoices that things are as they are. Hence his command.

God's search was an exhaustive one, such as mere man could not undertake. And David wants it so. He desires God thus to search him and to know him exhaustively, for then he is sure that God is what He claims to be. In the hands of his God, David is safe. Were God to act other than as He does and not to possess an exhaustive knowledge of David, then God would not be God, and there would be no use in having anything to do with him. When a man comes to know God as God is revealed in His Word he desires that God should search and try him, for such a desire is evidence of his need for God and also of his consecration to God.

In the first verse David had addressed God as LORD, now he speaks to Him as EL. Perhaps there is deliberateness in this choice of the word. In using it the Psalmist again brings to the fore the distinction between God and man. He wants the great God upon whose attributes he has been pondering to search him. Only this God can exhaustively know him, and hence he addresses God as EL.

In the first verse the Psalmist had declared that God had searched him and known. Now he reverts to that language, and in addition to the command to search him he commands God to know his heart. This time there is an object appended to the verb. It is not merely knowing as such, but the knowing of David's heart that is mentioned here.

As so often in the Bible, the heart is presented as the seat of the personality. If God knows David's heart, He will know David, for out of the heart are the issues of life. If the heart is planning evil and if its hatred is a wicked hatred, then God must know in order that David may be convicted of his sin. If the heart of David hates with a perfect hatred, then God must know. When a man can thus throw open his heart to God, as it were, he may be sure that his intentions are right. If there be wickedness within the heart God will convict him thereof. Well is it for us if we can appeal at all times to God to know our hearts whether there be integrity there or not.

Parallel to the first half of the verse is the second, 'Try me and know my inmost thoughts'. The root from which this last word ('disquieting thoughts') is derived basically means to branch out. Apparently the ramifications or branching out of thoughts is intended, so that the word actually refers to those thoughts which are disturbing or disquieting. Perhaps into his disturbed thought corruption and sin could most easily find an entrance. Even thoughts such as these must be tested of God. He must try them, examining them thoroughly so that they meet the tests which He imposes. If there be any evil even in these disturbing thoughts, God must convict David of that fact.

24. *And see if there be any wicked way in me, and lead me in the way everlasting.*

WHAT does David desire the Lord to find? The answer is clearly stated. If there is a way that leads to wickedness, it is that which God must find. Let us examine more closely the expression which the Psalmist actually employs. Some commentators, appealing to a somewhat similar word in Isaiah 48:5, believe that David is speaking of a way of idolatry, and is appealing to God to see whether there be any inclinations to idolatry within him. In answer to this, however, it has rightly been pointed out that inclinations toward or actual practice of idolatry could hardly be regarded as a secret sin of which David was unaware. Furthermore, the meaning 'idol' is really not justified here. It is something else of which David speaks.

The way of pain is the way that leads to pain and misery. It is a way that leads to inward punishments brought on by sin and also to outward punishments. In other words, it is the way that leads from God to the full recompense of sin, everlasting death. This way separates from God and leads one to a place where God's blessing is withdrawn.

Some commentators speak of the doctrine of the two ways which they think they find in the Psalms. It is true that this Psalm and the first Psalm together with other passages do refer to two ways. These two ways, however, do not have reference to some ordeal or cultic institution. Neither is the way of pain merely one that brings its own punishment with it, in distinction from an everlasting punishment. This way, rather, culminates in pain, from which there is no deliverance. If there is any such way within the Psalmist he desires God to see it.

On the other hand, he prays that God will lead him in the way everlasting. What, however, is meant by this language? Some think that the reference is to the way that is everlasting. In contrast to this it, is said, there is the way of the wicked, which will perish. David, on this interpretation, is praying that God will lead him in a way that does not perish but is everlasting. Again, others think that the reference is to a way that leads to everlasting life. Either of these is a possibility.

It may be that we cannot be dogmatic, but it is worthy of consideration to note that there is still another interpretation which has much to commend it. On this third view David is praying God to lead him in the old way, the way of former times. This would be the way that Abraham, Isaac and Jacob walked in. It is the way of the ancients of the people, and hence the way that has the favour of God upon it. Thus, it is the right way, that which leads unto eternal life. If David is led in the way of old, then he is in the way which will bring him into everlasting life.

And so it must be with us. Oh! that we might turn

from the superficiality of so much of present-day religious life and come once again to know God in His wondrous majesty! He is a Spirit, infinite, eternal and unchangeable in all of His glorious attributes. When we think upon these things, we must bow before Him in adoration and silence. He is God and we are but men. Before such a God the sinner cannot stand. He has no right. Yet we know that we are sinners, and that we have offended this holy God. May we, too, pray that He will search us and know our hearts and see if there be any wicked way within us! And if such a wicked way be found, may we lean upon His own mercy, provided for us in the gift of the Son of His love, even our Lord Jesus Christ, the only One who can lead us in the way everlasting.

SOME OTHER
BANNER OF TRUTH TRUST
TITLES

THE REFORMATION OF THE CHURCH

A selection of Reformed and Puritan documents, edited by Iain Murray

At a time when the Christian faith is commanding little influence in the nation, it may be regretted that the Church should be engaged with issues affecting her own life rather than the life of the masses of the people. Issues such as the Church-State relationship, the place of Episcopacy and the order and unity of the visible Church appear to be far removed from the urgent problem of the spiritual apathy of the average man and woman. But this is a shallow assessment. It is because of the prevailing religious apathy that the Church must set her own house in order.

Many of the ecclesiastical issues which are once more in prominence are subjects which have already been extensively dealt with in the literature of former centuries particularly in the Reformation and Puritan era. This book contains important selections from this literature as well as new translations from practically unknown Latin manuscripts. Each extract is preceded by an historical introduction.

The authors, extracts from whose writings are here reprinted, include Martin Luther, John à Lasco, John Hooper, William Tyndale, Thomas Shepard, John Owen, Jeremiah Burroughs, James Durham, William Cunningham and Charles Hodge. The subjects dealt with include: the Nature of the Church, the Regulative Principle, Things Indifferent, the Abolition of Vestments, Reforming the Church from Spiritual Corruptions, Episcopacy, Church and State, and the Government of the New Testament Church.

416 pages. Paperback, $2.50

JOHN G. PATON: MISSIONARY
TO THE NEW HEBRIDES

An autobiography, edited by his brother, James Paton

The autobiography of John G. Paton contains everything necessary to make it a missionary classic.

Born near Dumfries in 1824, of godly parents, Paton's early years were marked by a struggle against poverty. He was self-educated, and the training ground for his life's work was the slums of Glasgow where he laboured with success as a city missionary. With 'the wail of the perishing heathen in the South Seas' continually sounding in his ears, he prepared himself and was ordained as a missionary to the New Hebrides in 1858.

This group of thirty mountainous islands, so named by Captain Cook, with its unhealthy climate, was then inhabited by savages and cannibals of the worst kind. The first attempt to introduce Christianity to them resulted in John Williams and James Harris being clubbed to death within a few minutes of landing in 1839. The difficulties that confronted Paton were accentuated by the sudden death of his wife and child within months of their arrival.

Against the savagery and the superstition, despite the trials and the tragedies, Paton persevered and witnessed the triumph of the Gospel in two of these South Sea islands. His life is almost without parallel in missionary annals and his account of it is moving and gripping.

528 pages., $4.50

LECTURES ON REVIVALS

William B. Sprague

The subject of revival has become almost fashionable today. There is general agreement amongst Evangelicals that we need a revival. But there are many views as to what revival really is, how it may be promoted and what are the hindrances to it. Clear, scriptural and sanctified thinking and teaching on the subject is greatly needed.

This in the opinion of competent judges is just what Sprague provides. 'I consider Dr Sprague's volume', wrote John Angell James, the distinguished nonconformist leader of the last century, 'as the most important and satisfactory testimony that has yet reached us on the subject of revivals.' Charles Simeon, leader of the Evangelical party in the Church of England, inscribed in the flyleaf of his own copy, 'A most valuable book. I love the good sense of Dr Sprague.' Sprague's lectures ask and answer the questions which perplex us about revivals, as well as some which we are not, but should be, asking.

The volume is enhanced by the inclusion of letters to the author from twenty eminent American ministers, describing their own experiences of revivals and giving sound practical advice. Sprague, like them, is never dry or merely theoretical, because he lived at a time when the church in North America was being watered by the dew of heaven. The great object of his book was 'to vindicate and advance the cause of *genuine* revivals of religion'. All who have the same cause at heart may profit by reading this neglected volume.

472 pages., $3.50

C. H. SPURGEON: THE EARLY YEARS

The two most wonderful phenomena of the nineteenth century, it was once claimed, were Spurgeon in his *youth* and Gladstone in his *old age*. And truly, 'phenomenal' is the only word to describe the meteoric rise to fame of the youth who at 16 was 'the boy-preacher of the Fens,' and pastor of the Baptist Chapel, Waterbeach, while still in his teens. Called to New Park Street Chapel in 1854 when he was scarce 20, he took London by storm.

Unconventional in manner, aggressive in evangelism, preaching 'the old-fashioned Gospel,' Charles Haddon Spurgeon stood out in marked contrast to his contemporaries. The spiritual awakening which attended his preaching was, however, followed by uproar, ridicule and bitter opposition. His name was lampooned in the press and 'kicked about the street as a football.' Yet up to 10,000 flocked to hear him in the Surrey Gardens Music Hall on Sunday mornings; the circulation of his weekly printed sermons went up by leaps and bounds; he became the topic and theme of remark in all parts of the land, and even the subject of a leading article in *The Times*.

In the pages of Spurgeon's Autobiography these thrilling 'early years' are made to live again in a way no biographer could have done. His was no ordinary life and characteristically his own account of it is quite unique. The republication of this classic of spiritual history has long been overdue. Generously illustrated and carefully edited, this new edition of the first half of Spurgeon's Autobiography carries the story to 1859, the year of revival.

584 pages, 24 pages illustrations, $5.00

THE LIFE OF ELIJAH

A. W. PINK

The life of Elijah has gripped the thought and imagination of preachers and writers in all ages. His sudden appearance out of complete obscurity, his dramatic interventions in the national history of Israel, his miracles, his departure from earth in a chariot of fire, all serve to that end. Judgement and mercy were mingled throughout Elijah's astonishing career. From the moment when he steps forth, 'without father, without mother', 'as if he had been a son of the earth', to the day when his mantle fell from him and he crossed the river of death without tasting death, he exercised a ministry only paralleled by that of Moses, his companion of the Mount of Transfiguration.

It is fitting that the lessons which may be drawn from Elijah's ministry should be presented afresh to our generation. History repeats itself. The wickedness and idolatry rampant in Ahab's reign live on in our gross twentieth century's profanities and corruptions. Our lot is cast in a time of widespread and deep departure from the ancient landmarks of the people of the Lord. Truths dear to our evangelical forefathers have been trodden as the mire of the streets.

A. W. Pink's study of Elijah is particularly suited to the needs of the present day. He clearly felt called to the task of smiting the ungodliness of the age with the rod of God's anger. With this object he undertakes the exposition of Elijah's ministry and applies it to the contemporary situation.

320 pages, Paperback, $1.25

UNITY IN THE DARK

Donald Gillies

When Archbishop Fisher spoke of his forthcoming visit to the Pope in the Church Assembly on November 10th, 1960, he indicated that the conversations would not be kept secret. Yet when the meeting took place, nothing was disclosed. [*The Guardian*, November 11th and December 2nd, 1960.]

When it is asked what place the Pope would have in a United Church, Archbishop Ramsey says that this need not be settled until such a church is being formed. [*The Gospel and the Catholic Church*, p. 226.]

When the Queen was received by the Pope on May 5th, 1961, she wore a black dress and veil, yet Queen Fabiola of Belgium, a Catholic monarch, did not dress in this way for a similar reception. She wore white – like all Catholic Queens. No explanation was given in England, but Catholic countries took this as a sign of Protestant penitence.

In the 'Service of Reconciliation' [a prototype for other reunion services] outlined in the Anglican-Methodist Report it is proposed that each ministry receive the other by the laying on of hands. . . 'Then shall the bishop lay his hands on the head of each of the Methodist ministers in silence.' No explanation is given why such an act is needed, but it effectively serves to cover the Anglo-Catholic contention that episcopal ordination is necessary to a valid ministry.

This is the ecclesiastical spirit of the times in which we live. This is why a book like *Unity in the Dark* is needed.

128 pages, Paperback, 75 cents

THE MYSTERY OF PROVIDENCE

JOHN FLAVEL

Do we believe that everything in the world and in our own lives down to the minutest detail is ordered by the providence of God? Do we ever take time to observe and meditate on the workings of providence? If not, are we missing much? The Puritans, among others, would tell us we are.

It should be a delight and pleasure to us to discern how God works all things in the world for His own glory and His people's good. But it should be an even greater pleasure to observe the particular designs of providence in our own lives. 'O what a world of rarities', says John Flavel, 'are to be found in providence. . . . With what profound wisdom, infinite tenderness and incessant vigilance it has managed all that concerns us from first to last.' It was to persuade Christians of the excellency of observing and meditating upon this that Flavel first published his *Mystery of Providence* in 1678. Since then the work has gone through a number of editions and the Trust has published a paperback edition, slightly modernized in language and layout.

Based on the words 'God that performeth all things for me' (Ps. 57:2) this work shows us how Providence works for us in every stage and experience of our lives. The book is richly illustrated from the lives of believers and from the author's wide reading in church history. There are avenues of spiritual knowledge and experience opened to the Christian in this work which he probably never knew existed.

224 pages, Puritan paperback, $1.00

THE RARE JEWEL OF CHRISTIAN CONTENTMENT

JEREMIAH BURROUGHS

Jeremiah Burroughs (1599-1646) describes contentment as an inward, quiet and gracious frame of spirit which freely submits to and takes pleasure in God's disposal in every condition. He goes on to deal with the Mystery of Contentment, Lessons by which Christ teaches Contentment, the Excellence of Contentment, the Evils of a Murmuring Spirit, Aggravations of the Sin of Murmuring, the Excuses of a Discontented Heart and How to Attain Contentment. His grasp of doctrine, discernment into the very recesses of the human heart, comprehensive and profound knowledge of Scripture and ability to apply it, and superb gift of illustration are all exemplified in this book.

240 pages, Puritan paperback, $1.00